MAY ON MOTORS

James May

To Fusker

First published in this form in Great Britain in 2006 by
Virgin Books Ltd
Thames Wharf Studios
Rainville Road
London
W6 9HA

A catalogue record for this book is available from the British
Library.

ISBN 0 7535 1186 X
ISBN 9 780753 511862

The paper used in this book is a natural, recyclable product
made from wood grown in sustainable forests. The
manufacturing process conforms to the regulations of the
country of origin.

Typeset by TW Typesetting, Plymouth, Devon
Printed and bound in Great Britain by Bookmarque Ltd

CONTENTS

CONTENTS

INTRODUCTION: CAR FEVER

IT ALL STARTED WITH A MATCHBOX ASTON MARTIN

It really *did* start with a Matchbox Aston Martin. I was very small – no more than three years old – and asleep in bed. My dad had been away on a business trip of some sort and had bought the pocket-sized, iconic GT car (although this was long before the association with James Bond was cemented) as a sort of commemoration of his homecoming. I should have bought him one, I suppose, but he already had a real Ford Cortina.

The moment I woke up and found it on the pillow was, I think, the moment I realised that I was deeply interested in cars.

Then again, every small boy I've ever met, and even quite a few girls, like playing with toy cars, so that supposedly seminal, die-cast revelation is hardly a good excuse for making a living from writing about them. In fact, I'm absolutely amazed that it's even possible.

Driving around in cars is not exactly the exclusive preserve of a few, in the way that walking on the moon or being a member of Pink Floyd is. The vast majority of adults is entirely familiar with the process. Yet there are no regular newspaper or magazine columns given over to Buzz Aldrin or Roger Waters, while acres of space are still devoted to people who drive about in cars. Why? Why are there no weekly columns about washing up or laundry? They are no less remarkable. It's not as if I have to be possessed of remarkable insight to find something to say about motoring. All of my friends have opinions on the subject. In fact, when they have a really good one, I write it down and use it in a column.

Let's imagine my dad had come home with a microscope instead. I might well have become very interested in bacteria or the shape of sugar crystals. My mate Cookie *did* have a microscope, and was. However, he didn't slip unwittingly into an adult life of trying to find something droll to say about bacteria or the shape of sugar crystals. He eventually threw the microscope in the back of a cupboard and found a job in banking.

It's not even as if there's that much to say about cars *per se*, the whole business being so well understood. This is both a hardship and a great relief. Every motoring columnist sits down in front of the blank screen with its mocking cursor in the top left-hand corner and thinks, 'Right. What can I write that's really interesting without having to think of too much to say about the bloody car?' The benefit to you, I hope, is that motoring columns are full of surprises and rarely about cars.

So I could, of course, argue that driving and the possession of a car is actually a window on to some deeper and less well-charted region of the human condition. But I won't, because that would be pretentious crap, which is something to be avoided. Sooner or later I'm going to have to admit that I just like cars and that I've wasted a life that could have been spent gainfully employed in direct marketing.

*   *   *

So I'm afraid to have to tell you, reader, that you've just bought a book about cars, for which I should probably apologise. In my defence, however, I have never written anything that wasn't intended to be read on the lavatory. So I hope that's where you'll keep this book.

POLITICS AND MORALITY

SOME HOT AIR ON THE ETHICAL ISSUE OF AIRBAGS

D arwin would worry. Sure, the painfully slow process of natural selection, which makes even the development of the Porsche 911 look rapid, has been largely circumvented by developed man. We can interfere with the copulating habits of horses to produce an exceptionally swift one for the track or a sturdy beast to haul the plough, and we have largely outwitted those diseases whose toll on humanity was considered by Darwin's inspiration, Malthus, to be necessary for the control of the population. But segregating mankind for the purposes of procreation can only lead to disaster, as a quick glance at the Royal Family reveals. Likewise, granting certain people special privileges where survivability is concerned is likely to cause problems.

With that in mind, the latest developments in airbag technology can only be viewed with misgiving. 'Your passenger's life is not an option,' trumpets Honda, revealing that it is the latest maker to offer a passenger's bag as standard, on the Civic five-door. The implication is that it is thrown in gratis, that Honda is taking an egalitarian stance on life preservation. Very laudable.

But who most needs this airbag? Not the occupant of a brilliantly engineered, ABS-braked and ultimately progressively crumpling Honda; it is poor sods such as I, lashed behind the hard, spindly wheel of my '67 Triumph Vitesse or '70 Rover P6, against whose unyielding columns I am the more likely to be unwittingly dashed by deficiencies in the handling and braking departments. Yet an airbag remains resolutely absent from the options list of cars that need one most.

The problem is that to acquire the airbag – any airbag, in fact – you first have to buy a new or nearly-new car, and only a certain sector of society enjoys that privilege. A social imbalance of Darwinian implications looms: all road users share danger equally, yet the selection system is being manipulated in favour of the survival – and hence procreation – of a specific group. Taking this idea to its extreme, the most likely survivors of a Malthusian population-pruning scenario based on roads rather than disease are the drivers of weighty, voluminous and multiple-airbagged off-road vehicles. Clearly, this does not bode well for the species.

But, fellow paupers, those of you whom Malthus would have eradicated by TB, fear not. I have had an idea. It came to me at a recent lunch, where some boffin was talking bullishly of the latest thinking in 'peripheral airbag technology'. We already have airbags in the seats; now there is a move towards airbags in the doors, airbags in the back, airbags in the roof and, for all I know, an airbag in the boot to protect your shopping. Why not, I thought, airbags in the bumpers, triggered by a simple radar device the instant before a collision and thus allowing cars to bounce harmlessly off each other? But that would still leave our favourite safety feature firmly welded to new-car purchase. And then it came to me. The airbag should not be fitted in any of these places; it should not, in fact, be fitted to the car at all.

The airbag should be worn by the driver. This is a precept of glaring apparency onto which the motor industry has completely failed to cotton.

May's Acme Airbag Shirt (pat. pend.) has numerous advantages over traditional airbags, not least of which is that it allows all people to benefit from life-saving technologies hitherto the preserve of wealthy new-car buyers, thus levelling the survivability playing field once again. It is not without precedent, either – on a Boeing 747 you will find an individual lifejacket under your seat, not one giant one attached to the aeroplane and inflated by a red toggle in the cockpit. Furthermore, as the trunk forms the main bulk of the body, the bag in the Acme Shirt (or Bagshirt, as it will come to be known) will automatically be tailored to suit the weight and dimensions of the wearer. How will it work? Allow me to, er, expand.

The only part of an airbag that needs to be attached to the car is the sensor that measures the severity of retardation in an impact: it is mere idleness of thought that sees the bag itself stuffed into the steering wheel or glovebox along with it. The Bagshirt will come with a small, self-adhesive sensor unit, to be attached to any part of the car that will not deform in an accident – say the dashboard of the Triumph or anywhere aft of the front bumper on the Rover. The sensor is connected to the bag and detonator in the shirt by a coaxial wire like the one on your Walkman headphones – thus the whole enjoys universal compatibility with any car.

Indeed, once the airbag has been separated from the car its applications are endless. The fitment of a manual override ripcord makes the shirt attractive to public transport users, pedestrians and even the likes of window cleaners who absent-mindedly step back to admire their work.

Stylish, versatile and discreet, the Bagshirt adapts to any health and safety scenario and protects you from the moment you get dressed until you return to the safety of your bed. For cyclists, to whom lightweight and sartorial absurdity seem to be of paramount importance, I have devised an airbag headband. This not only looks even more stupid than a polystyrene helmet, it offers the added benefit of preventing cyclists' heads from damaging the bodywork of cars.

Apart from the difficulty of finding a backer, there remains only the small problem of legislation. The Bagshirt is open to abuse so, as with the emergency cord on the train, there would have to be penalties for improper use. There will be plenty of opportunities for that, such as down the pub last night, trying to enjoy a quiet pint when that bloke from round the corner came over, breathed cheese and onion in my face and started talking about his Caterham again . . .

Dunno, officer. I was just standing there talking and my airbag went off.

AH, MR BOND – WE WEREN'T EXPECTING YOU TO DO THAT

I may have given an impression to the contrary in the past, but I'm really not averse to the idea of European unity. As a business arrangement, it's a great thing – if it makes it easier to truck a load of Melton Mowbray pork pies to a Belgian supermarket and sell them, then that can't be bad.

But the notion that the peoples of Europe can become subsumed into some amorphous *Homo Continentalis* is deeply offensive to me and, I suspect, to our neighbours too, and I find attempts to Europeanise things a bit insulting. Remember, it's because of Europe that the Marathon bar became Snickers and the label in your Marks & Spencer's underpants says 'cotton/coton' for the benefit of French people who can't fathom out the English word.

I like national stereotypes. They're fun and, in the final analysis, often not that wide of the mark. I don't mind that Italians think I buy condoms in packs of twelve so I have one for every month of the year, and in return I expect to be allowed to think that all Italians are mad and that the whole of Italy is *chiuso* whenever I go there on holiday. I expect Frenchmen to have a profound and chauvinistic love of France, even if I can't fathom it, and look, Jerry, I know we're always banging on about the war but it's the last significant thing we did. You could learn to take yourself a bit less seriously. You did lose after all.

So as the House of Commons vigorously debates the pros and cons of a single European currency, I wonder if our honourable members could take a little time to discuss something with far greater implications – the Euro Bond. I'm talking about Bond, James Bond. For in his new film, *Goldeneye*, our hero may well be wearing Church's brogues but he will also be flouncing about in Italian designer suits. He may even eat croissants for breakfast for all I know. And though his personal car will be his old Aston Martin DB5 from the *Goldfinger* days, guess what car Q will provide for Bond's mission to the Bahamas to blow everything up? Why, a BMW Roadster. *Aber ja, natürlich.*

I know it's not my job to tell Albert R Broccoli how to make his films any more than it's his to ring up and tell me what to write in my humble column, but – do pay attention, Cubby – double-oh *seben* is no longer just a fictional film character, he is an ambassador for a certain British stereotype that may not exist in reality but which is greatly admired the world over, especially in the States. Nice though the BMW is, Bond simply cannot drive it any more than Douglas Bader could join the Luftwaffe in a film about the Battle of Britain.

'The Roadster,' puffs BMW, 'reflects the essence of James Bond – smart, a little audacious and always in control of the situation'. Well, excuse me but Bond, as I remember him, is not 'a little audacious'. He is an elitist, a cad and a complete bounder, and it is these qualities that should be reflected in his car. It just so happens that an appropriate one is available and from the marque that so excellently provided for the best Bond (Connery) in the best Bond film (*Goldfinger*). That car is the Aston Martin DB7. Now there's a motor for the kind of bloke who regards seduction as something he must 'do for England'.

I happen to know that Aston came close to a deal on the *Goldeneye* film. The producers had even got as far as specifying an interior trim to match Bond's Italian wardrobe when suddenly, and for reasons United Artists won't reveal, it was over to BMW and, for Aston, goodbye, Mr Bond. Newport Pagnell must be hopping mad. The release of the film in November would have coincided nicely with its efforts to promote the DB7 in the States, and that, too, would have been good for what Lord Young used to call UK PLC. And if not the Aston then why not a supercharged Jag or even a rorty TVR, in some ways a spiritual descendant of the original DB Astons? This is a matter of national prestige worthy of attention from Bond himself, except that he seems to have gone a bit soft.

Perhaps the new Bond is a vegetarian. Perhaps he will slip into his leather sandals and chunky sweater and set off to battle against the dark forces of sexual inequality. But that wouldn't be quite right, and neither is the BMW. Bond in a Beemer is like Byron in Esperanto. Next thing you know is he won't have his dinner jacket on under the wet suit.

I'm not sure I'll be going to see *Goldeneye* in November. As a fan of Bond, a lover of British cars and a patriot, I think it will annoy me. I mean, do I really expect a BMW-driving European 007 to endear himself to a fan club of stuffy, pompous, stereotypical old British farts like me?

No, Mr Bond – I expect you to die.

JESUS CHRIST – THE WAY THAT BLOKE DRIVES IS BEYOND BELIEF

A mate of mine is entering a competition to win a Mini. The first bit, where you have to match road signs to pictures of junctions, is easy, but even four pints couldn't flush out a satisfactory tie-breaker. What innovation or initiative, it asks, would do most to improve road safety?

I don't think he'll win; not even if he tippexed out my idea when he got home and wrote 'airbag' instead. I fear the judges will be looking for the current perceived wisdom on road safety, which goes something like *raise driving standards by introducing a tougher driving test with regular re-tests every ten years*. That, in fact, is smack on the fifteen-word allowance. But though that might win a Mini, it's not the answer.

I've met a lot of people who support a harder driving test, and I expect they could all pass it, too. And yet many of them are the sort of drivers in whose cars I hesitate to tread and to whom I most certainly would not lend mine. Their abilities behind the wheel are beyond compare, but safe driving has little to do with skill and everything to do with attitude, and you can't test for that. So the roads are full of ditherers, but so what? You know when someone is about to do something dozy, yet how many drivers deliberately allow an awkward or even dangerous situation to develop so that they can lean on the horn and enjoy a moment of self-righteous indignation? An emphasis on driving skill leads to arrogance and elitism among those who think they've got it. With all due acknowledgement of my own sanctimoniousness, what's needed is a healthy dose of humility. Safe driving is not about being good but about knowing just how bad you really are.

On the roads, courtesy and humility are about as evident as Talbot Tagoras. Back to that tie-breaker then – what eminent body could take the initiative of promoting a bit of common decency? The government? I don't think so. The Royal Family might have been up to it once, but not in its new role as the nation's tackiest soap. I was wrestling with this one when I was cut up by a cyclist wearing a jacket bearing the embroidered legend 'Don't follow me, follow Jesus'. There was no disputing the first part of his edict, as he proceeded to ride across the pavement and into a shopping arcade, but, nevertheless, I think he had the answer. The perfect model for road safety already exists in good old-fashioned, God-fearing, fire-and-brimstone Christianity.

Hey, don't turn over. I'm not one of those guys you come across when channel-hopping on a Sunday morning, I'm not wearing a brown cable-knit jumper as I write this and I couldn't play 'Lord of the Dance' on the guitar to save my life, let alone my soul. But it's on the roads that we will see again the value of Jesus' teachings. Providing you're prepared to be a bit ecumenical with the truth, they can be readily interpreted as parables on road safety. Did He not scold the rich Pharisee Simon for making Him unwelcome in his house, blessing instead the poor woman who bathed His tired feet with her tears? And would not a little similar humility improve traffic flow and defuse aggression? If a Samaritan could save the life of a sworn enemy, surely to God we can forgive people who merely pull out in front of us? And it is the repentant tax collector, not the arrogant man who believes he's a good Christian, who earns Jesus' forgiveness. The meek, then, shall inherit the road.

Apart from anything else, Christianity needs a bit of a rethink. Hardly anybody goes to church these days (except Japanese tourists) and a few months ago the foundation received a further blow when the infamous Rev. Antony Freeman was caught preaching to his dwindling flock that, er, there isn't a God. The General Synod, itself unsure of its exact position on God these days, felt it necessary to debate this at great length before throwing him out, but then that's hardly surprising when another C of E bigwig comes on Radio 4 and talks of 'faithless Christianity'.

Those ministers who lament the declining authority of the church should shake off their stuffy cassocks (I was a choirboy, so I know what it's like in there) and take religion on to the roads of Britain. If the Messiah comes again this Christmas, He will arrive by car.

I tested the new faith over two weeks during which I had to drive the same journey to and from the office every day. For the first week, I was the devil's own driver. Nobody was allowed to overtake me, nobody joined a queue in front of me, pedestrians remained marooned in the middle of the road and if anyone gave me so much as a look, I gave 'em the finger.

For week two I was Christian Motorist, and all went before me, for he who is last shall be first. And it came to pass that a taxi driver fell upon me from behind, and he was sorely wrath and worshipped false gods upon the loud trumpet, saying unto me that I shall beget no children and that my seed shall be spilled fruitlessly in the wilderness, if you see what I mean. But I heeded him not. And lo! The journey times were no longer but I went in peace, knowing that God's in his heaven and all's right with the world.

No, I don't think Gideon's bible in the glovebox will win the Mini, and the judges' decision is final. But come the final judgement, perhaps I'll be rewarded in heaven.

THIS MAN'S DRIVING LIKE AN IDIOT – HE MUST BE STARVING

Ask yourself this simple question: which is more important, a man's life or Chicken Tikka Bhuna?

Well the votes are streaming in and the swingometer is moving decisively to the right. It's too early to be absolutely certain but it would appear that the constituency of *Car* readers has voted unanimously for the human existence. It looks as if you alone have voted for curry, Mr May. Any comment on that?

Well, it's easy to be sanctimonious when you're sitting nice and comfy in your armchair, reclining in the bath or perhaps settling in for a long stretch of solitary confinement in the smallest room. But now put yourself in the position I was in when I was dropped, unsuspecting, into this dark and uncharted corner of the moral maze.

I had just returned from some culinarily bankrupt country like France and was looking forward to a meal of honest, hearty British cooking. My alimentary canal had attained the status of favourite organ and as I drove the gentle two miles home from the Light of Nepal, breathing deeply of the Empire's most enduring legacy, I allowed my mind to wander and then dwell on one of the sweet mysteries that attend the cult of curry.

Such as how, if you strike a whole poppadom with a clenched fist, one of the resulting pieces – it may be as large as your hand or it may be a tiny fragment retrieved with a wetted pinkie – but *one* of them will always be in the shape of India. *Always*. And how if you break that piece, you will still find another, smaller India; and so, I believe, it must go on until you arrive at the atom. And then some worthless drunkard stepped into the road right in front of me.

I braked. Of course I braked, it was pure instinct. But it was merely the driving instinct, and within a fraction of a

second – and we're talking about the sort of timespan your
ABS deals in here – a stronger, more deeply rooted one, the
survival instinct of the hunter/gatherer, took over. From the
corner of my eye I had seen the brown bag begin to topple.
I released the brakes thus condemning the witless buffoon
before me to certain death. I caught his uncomprehending
eye with mine and braked again, but by now the physics of
the curry instability problem were becoming very compli-
cated, the whole bag beginning the second of its metro-
nomic oscillations, but the less heavily damped sauce within
probably on its third. These two frequencies, I dimly knew,
could conspire to hurl the whole lot onto the floor, and man
cannot live by nan bread alone. I released the brakes.

Now he was hopping, skipping and stumbling sideways
along the road, vainly trying to fend off a huge Ford with a
limp hand. I cadence braked in a desperate attempt to bring
the rapid cycle of stop-and-go into opposite phase with the
bhuna-bag's swayings until, as it reached its greatest rear-
wards deflection, I stabbed home the pedal and came to a
halt with everything still upright. Looking up, I was further
encouraged to discover that my victim, in medical parlance,
was shaken but unhurt.

Good God; I had weighed a man's life against my next
meal and the alarmingly pale upholstery of the Ultima-spec
Galaxy had almost tipped the balance in favour of the food.
It seems unthinkable now, but in that terrifying instant
when I reverted to the Neanderthal his life meant nothing
to me – it was but one grain in a sea of pilau – and my
dinner was everything.

Still appalled? Who hasn't pulled away from the garage
forecourt and immediately inserted the tantalisingly crimped end of a Ginster's pasty into the mouth, only to find it
coming apart at the soft underbelly, leaving you in need of
two hands to stem the egress of filling, and driving the next
two miles in first gear at 8,000 rpm? Who hasn't resorted to

steer-by-knee at motorway speeds to do battle with a recalcitrant crisp bag?

Speed does not kill, using a mobile phone while driving is no more hazardous than smoking or listening to the radio, and the fatuous press release from some safety organisation urging me to MOT myself before taking the wheel is a nonsense. For the most dangerous driver on the road is the one with an empty belly. Next time you're thinking about using the car, don't ask yourself whether you're fit to drive, think when you last had a good square meal.

WELSH, THE MYSTICAL AND ANCIENT LANGUAGE OF ROAD SIGNS

The other day I heard on the radio that, somewhere in Brazil, an area of natural beauty the size of Wales has just been destroyed. This isn't the first time this has happened. A similar report comes out about once a year.

And, once a year, some wag in a pub somewhere will say 'Why couldn't it just have been Wales?'

Well, it wasn't me. For some reason, I've spent much of the last two weeks motoring in Wales and I have to say I've come away rather liking the place. Wales is a land of Dafydils; of green valleys and gentle hills. Of Port Talbot steelworks too, but as they make the sheet metal for your fridge, your washing machine and quite possibly your car, this is a good thing.

The Welsh all seem to drive old Ford Fiestas at about 25 mph, but so what? Provided you're in a Nissan 350Z, as I was, it's a simple matter to drop down a couple of cogs, fly past and continue marvelling at a view of the world pretty much as Adam would have known it.

Now you're expecting me to say something like *the only problem with Wales is that it's full of Welsh people*. But, again, I'm going to have to disappoint you. They may say 'there's lovely' rather too often and they do seem to be more susceptible to being ginger than the rest of us, but we can hardly hold that against them. In any case, there are only a few hundred Welsh people, and most of them seem to be either in the pub or at choir practice. Or learning Welsh.

I wonder if there is anyone in the world who can only speak Welsh. Presumably there is. Why else would a cash machine ask you to 'choose your language' and then offer only English and Welsh? Fair enough. If a bunch of pasty-faced ginger separatists insist on conversing only in their native tongue, then that's their look-out.

For the rest of us, meanwhile, it's baffling and even dangerous.

In other European countries, it is always possible to find some common ground between a new word you see on a sign and one you already know; so in Italy, *curva pericolosa* obviously means 'dangerous bends'. Walk into a Welsh hotel, however, and though the sign in reception may be imagined to say 'welcome', it looks more like an insult. Maybe it is. There is no way of knowing, because Welsh has nothing in common with any other language I know of.

Of course, similar difficulties are experienced by travellers in Japan, but that's different. Japan isn't in England, and Wales is.

Here, for example, is a Welsh coastal road sign: *Pergyl – ochrau dibyn*. It means 'Danger – cliff edges'. Yet elsewhere on the same prom is a sign saying *Dim nofio ger y creigau* – No swimming near the cliff. Now both of these signs include a word for 'cliff', yet they have no word in common. How can that be? I know Wales has a lot of coastline but having more than one official word for 'cliff' strikes me as asking for trouble.

Out on the road, the visiting motorist will endure yet more confusion. Motorway services are the *gwasanaethau*, but by the time I'd worked that out I'd already overshot. The next *gwasanaethau* wasn't for another 35 miles, and I was desperate for a leek.

'Please drive slowly' appears first as *gyrrwch yn ofalus*, but by then you're through the village anyway. And I'm not even going to attempt to translate 'road liable to flooding'. It was something so enormous that it required a second, huge sign. Good news for the sheet metal producers at Port Talbot, I suppose, but less good for the residents of the nearby hamlet, who are now shrouded in eternal night.

The impression is that some nationalists have loaded a blunderbuss with consonants and then rampaged around the land firing indiscriminately at the road furniture. In some places I saw electronic dot-matrix signs presumably updated from some central nerve centre. After the third or fourth I concluded that Evans must have nodded off with his face resting on the keyboard.

But the Welsh problem is at its most acute on the country's many winding roads, and especially on the approach to a treacherous bend (of which there are many in the hills). In Cornwall, Yorkshire or even Scotland, the legend SLOW would be writ large upon the tarmac as a warning. It's writ large in Wales, too.

But first, it says *ARAF*. And by the time you've thought 'Gosh, I wonder what *araf* means', it's already too late.

And then your Nissan 350Z ends up in a ditch.

(Letters of complaint from Welsh readers should be addressed to Motoring at the *Daily Telegraph*. In English.)

SOME BLUE-CHIP BULLSHIT FROM THE MARKETING MEN

The other day, a man from Mercedes-Benz said something very strange to me. Explaining why the long-wheelbase A-class had been extended by 170 mm, he said it was 'designed to appeal to those customer groups interested in more space-oriented concepts'.

I wrote this down and smuggled it home with me. Then I rang directory enquiries to get the number for Bletchley Park, but discovered that it had closed down in the 40s. In any case, I was informed, someone had nicked the Enigma machine.

There was nothing for it but to apply my own decrypting skills to this apparently meaningless string of letters. Long into the night I toiled with dictionary and thesaurus and eventually, as the candle spluttered towards extinction, I had it cracked. Ha! This new A-class was *for people who wanted something bigger.*

It wasn't code at all, it was just marketing, the art of stating the bleedin' obvious in as convoluted a way as possible. And I've finally had enough of it.

In fact I've been feeling this way for some years but have so far hesitated to say anything for fear of alienating quite a few people who I would count amongst my friends. Now, though, I've decided that it's all their fault for not getting a proper job. Marketing is first-rate, premium-brand cobblers. I am amazed to learn that some of these people have a degree in marketing, which amounts to a first-class honours in waffle from the University of Whittering.

In fairness, I have met one or two marketing executives from the motor industry who talk plain good sense. At the recent launch of the X-Type, Jaguar's John Able stood up and spoke almost entirely in the language of Keats and Byron. But this is rare. All too often I am assailed with guff about how many A-levels the prospective owners will have, or about how the customer profile embraces the active lifestyle and the needs of the young and young-at-heart. If there were such a thing as a Marketing-English/English-Marketing dictionary, everything in it would be translated as *cf: horse's arse*.

The Jaguar man was actually talking about *sales*, which is what marketing is really about and a perfectly worthy pursuit. Unfortunately, though, most marketing people are far too middle-class to admit that they're in the business of peddling stuff, so they dress it up as a cod philosophy instead. They somehow imagine that the genius of Beethoven can be reduced to a few fatuous 'attributes', which could then be fed into a Palm Pilot to produce another nine symphonies.

'The brand,' they're always telling me, 'is everything'. This is the biggest chunk of blue-chip balderdash out there. The product is everything. The BMW brand is revered across the world because it appears on the bonnets of some very fine motor cars. Start sticking the same propeller symbol on a series of unreliable rust buckets and the cars would not suddenly be perceived as great; no, the BMW name would be destroyed. Look what happened to Jaguar in the 70s – the most evocative brand in motoring was worth the square root of sod all whilst it was in the hands of resentful communists. And contrary to popular opinion there is nothing wrong with the Marks & Spencer brand; it's just a sign above the door and the only time there's anything wrong with it is when one of the light bulbs blows to give us Marks 'n' Sparks. The root of the retailer's recent problems has been that there's something wrong with the clothes. Except the pants, which are still excellent.

The marketing mentality is, in my view, at the root of this country's dumbing-down problem. There are too many people with marketing backgrounds controlling television and publishing. Government is marketed. Projects such as the Millennium Dome fail because they rely on too much corporate sponsorship, and corporate sponsorship puts them in the hands of marketing people who ultimately insult your intelligence, because they somehow imagine they're being very clever and you're very stupid. Speaking personally, the opposite is obviously true – that's why I have an influential column in the august journal *Top Gear* and they're all poncing about with pie charts and PowerPoint presentations.

The truth is that far too many people in marketing are those who didn't have sufficient talent or imagination to find proper creative work in the media or advertising, and I'm sick of them treating me like a halfwit. On a car launch I'd rather talk to engineers and boffins. I know they have some strange ideas about sports jackets and an overt fondness for the 0.0005 mm Rotring Propelling Pencil, but in the end anyone who understands the workings of a diesel injector down to the last few microns of its tolerances is going to be stimulating company, because engineering is a true and exact science enlivened with an occasional burst of pure artistry. Marketing is just rubbish.

But, fortunately, it won't last. The mistake marketing has made is the one made by the used car business – it has revealed too much of its own workings to the people. Words such as 'aspirational' 'attribute' and 'awareness' are already entering the common language in their marketing usage, and most people are beginning to understand how brands are being manipulated in an attempt to fool them into thinking they are buying 'exclusivity' or a 'premium product'.

Next, everyone will start to question all this, then they will realise that it's all nonsense, and that, finally, will be the end of marketing. Good.

FOR PETE'S SAKE GO OUT AND CATCH SOME RAPISTS

Some weeks ago, in this column, I made some cheap cracks about Welsh road signs, and as a result was sentenced to death in my absence by the Welsh National Assembly.

I am now prepared to retract my comments, but on one condition. Wales can keep its multi-lingual roadsigns – *da nhw*[1] – but in return must also agree to keep its chief constable Richard Brunstrom, who I'm disappointed to learn is English.

Mr Brunstrom, who is also head of road policing at the police, has annoyed everyone (but especially the Welsh) in the past with his uncompromising stance on speed enforcement. But now, in a further attempt to disguise his force's dismal record on burglary detection, he has decided to target old people as well.

He's backing a new device called the impairment-o-meter, which will be used to test old folks' reaction times at the roadside. Little is known about the constable's evil machine, other than that it is a hand-held instrument that will require its victim to make push-button responses to some sort of visual challenge. Something similar was a feature of fun fairs when I was a lad, only now it's being used to tyrannise your aged parents.

'When you get older, your brain cells die and your body is slowly shutting down,' says Brunstrom. 'We know tiredness is a problem, but we don't yet know the impact of age. We need to find out.'

Well, if he spent more time out on the beat he'd know perfectly well the impact of age on driving: wearing a hat, sitting too close to the wheel, owning a Honda Accord for twenty years and keeping it suspiciously clean, buying a hard-backed road atlas, and completing five laps of the M25

---

[1] Good for them.

before working out which exit to take. This sort of thing is great for more cheap gags but as far as I can make out none of it is a serious threat to road safety.

Ah, you're thinking: but old people drive very slowly. So? Wait for a clear, straight stretch, drop it down a cog and overtake in accordance with the police Roadcraft system of car control. And if they happen to be driving as slowly as Mary Limond, a 75-year-old who was recently fined £200 and given 6 penalty points for driving at 5 mph, you could jog alongside and regale them with stories about the blitz.

I find the Mrs Limond case curious. She says she was driving slowly because she had new glasses and was having difficulty adjusting to them at dusk. So, surely, slowing down was the right thing to do. We'd be expected to slow down in fog, because visibility is reduced. Visibility was reduced on whatever evening Mrs Limond was driving – it's just that it was only reduced in her car.

We're fined for driving a bit too fast, and fined for driving too slowly. Not so long ago the police were telling us that young drivers were dangerous, but now it's old ones. My insurance company tells me I'm a high risk because I work in the media and I'm not married. If this sort of thing goes on we will arrive at a situation in which unless you're a 38-year-old married accountant with two children driving a Volvo estate at 29 mph, you may as well go straight down the station and hand yourself in.

Apart from anything else, picking on old people is dreadfully un-British. So their brain cells are dying off? I'm fairly confident that I haven't generated any new ones recently, and neither, I suspect, has the chief constable. We can accommodate the trifling shortcomings of the elderly, if only because none of us is getting any younger.

Some old boy may be taking an inordinately long time to negotiate a mini roundabout, but for all we know he may once have had the steady hand and razor-sharp reactions necessary to plant a bouncing bomb on the face of the Eider Dam. In which case he's entitled to dither about in a Nissan Micra during his twilight years.

It's time for the rest of us to stick up for our senior citizens, and for my part I'd like to help them prepare for the impairment-o-meter, slated for introduction in 2006. My guess is that the machine will present an unfinished sentence and a choice of two concluding words, the right one of which has to be selected with a button before the arresting officer can say 'You're nicked, Grandad.' Practise on this example to avoid being prematurely banged up in a rest home.

Eeeh, bloody hell, policemen these days look so . . .
(A) Young
(B) Old

(Richard Brunstrom is 50).

BUYING A HOUSE? BUY A CAR INSTEAD

Let's hear it for the motor trade. What a smashing bunch of blokes they are (none of them seem to be women).

I mention this because of the activities of two of my good friends this week. One is thinking of buying a new car, so I've been tagging along with him to various dealers, he being of the belief that I know what I'm doing. In truth, I've never actually bought a brand new car, although in fairness I have bought quite a few brand new motorcycles, which amounts to the same experience only with less carpet in the showroom.

Another chum has moved house today, although when I say 'today' what I mean is that he's just resolved a process that's been going on for what seems like years. Observing his eternal suffering, and leafing through the heaving file of admin that accompanied the buying of my own house in an attempt to help him out, has persuaded me to reassess my opinion of our brave lads on the nation's forecourts.

You see, some years ago a very authoritative survey of the British public revealed that most of you would rather go to the dentist than visit a car showroom. If, as you read this, you happen to be sitting on an upturned packing case under a single 40-watt bulb, clutching a knackered kettle and wondering how you're ever going to get rid of the smell of aftershave, you should find this sentiment truly remarkable. A car may be in second place in the hierarchy of financial commitment for most of us, but buying one is like going out for an ice cream compared with the league-topping transaction that is securing somewhere to sleep.

It's nearly five years since I moved house, but I'm still reeling from the experience. These days, you can walk into a Ford dealership with little more than a pair of your old pants and drive away in a new Fiesta. But the instant you slap the 'for sale' sign outside your existing property, an ugly mob queues up from your door to eternity, all wanting to take your money in return for doing the square root of sod all.

You can go to a good car dealership and be quoted a price for the car in the window; taxed, registered, full of fuel, engine running and ready to drive away. However you want to pay – cash, deposit and finance, part-exchange, lease plan, whatever – the salesman can come up with the figures in a blur of index finger and calculator. But make an offer on a house, have it accepted, and after that the cogs on the adding machine go into overdrive.

Where, for example, did my solicitor's charge of £165 for phone calls and faxes come from? I can't spend that much on phone calls in a month, and my phone is smouldering from overuse. Apart from anything else, I don't remember him ringing me. I always had to ring him and he was never, ever in. Never.

Meanwhile, within seconds of entering the average car showroom, you will meet a man who is almost impossible to shake off, even if you've turned up at the Porsche garage in your decorating trousers. If you have a vague interest in a car and can produce a driving licence, you can usually go for a test drive. The first two times I came to view my new home, the estate agent couldn't even find the key to the garage.

The other day, for example, I found myself in a VW dealership with mate no 1, poking around a line of nearly new Golfs. I deliberately baited the salesman with questions about engines and specs, but however much I thought I knew about Golfs, he knew three times as much. A surveyor, on the other hand, will send you a bill for £500 and tell you that your prospective home probably won't fall down. But then again, he will point out, it might. Who knows? He obviously doesn't.

I reckon the business of conveyancing is at least thirty years behind motor trading. I notice that the solicitor wrote to me with a typewriter. He didn't take credit cards so I had to pay my own bank for the privilege of sending him a big pile of money by something called 'electronic transfer'. It's right up there with the Telex machine and phones whose mouthpieces and earpieces are separate items. I bought my last motorcycle with a switch card, over the phone.

The motor trade has regularly come in for a hard time. I dare say it has its charlatans, but it has, overall, shown itself to be a transparent and competitive business that can be beaten into shape by the consumer, as is right and proper. House buying is just a racket.

And you should see the wallpaper in mate no 2's new sitting room. It's bloody horrible.

HOW THE MEN OF BRITAIN BETRAYED THEMSELVES

Some weeks ago I wrote to you all, via this newspaper column, seeking help with a manly dilemma. Should I sell my old BSA motorcycle? And if I should, by what means? And then, most importantly, there was the issue of whether I should use the money to buy some carpet for my stairs or another, more modern bike.

To help you to help me, I provided an executive-style tick-box decision tree diagram and invited you to fill it in and send it to me, although I never imagined anyone actually would. There is always something more pressing than this sort of thing and in any case, it would mean having to find a post office in order to buy a stamp.

Well, the response has been enormous. So enormous, in fact, that any intention to reply to you all individually soon went the way of any correspondence that advised me to buy the carpet, ie out of the window.

There were quite a few offers of nearly-new Triumphs at tempting prices. There were also some very imaginative solutions I hadn't considered, including some investment plans and the offer of a bungalow, which would negate the stair carpet issue altogether. Someone suggested turning the old Beeza into an artwork and yet another bloke simply wrote and told me to pull myself together.

I have to say I'm deeply flattered by all this. I think it may be a mark of the British people's greatness that even with the Iraq War, the European Constitution, rising interest rates and the threat of some football, they can still find time to pause and help a chap at one of the crossroads of his life.

In the end you decreed, by a slim majority, that I should chop in the BSA (part-exchange value £2,000) for a new Triumph Bonneville. So I sold it on eBay for £1,800 and spent half the money on a 1978 Moto Guzzi T3 California that has been left in a shed for eighteen years and doesn't work. The other half has been put aside for 'maintenance'. So there you have it. I've wasted your time and I apologise.

On the other hand, something very useful has come out of all this. Because my postbag reveals that for decades hapless men who are now wracked by remorse have been cajoled by their womenfolk into flogging their motorcycles to pay for carpet, cookers, and other fashionable domestic trappings whose appeal is fleeting. This has got to stop.

I thought the emasculation of men was a fairly recent phenomenon, what with rumours of declining sperm counts, the advent of the lifestyle vehicle, hair products brazenly designed for 'men' and the rise of the so-called 'metrosexual'. But now I realise that it has been going on since at least the 30s, when some poor sod was bludgeoned into pawning off his flat-twin Douglas to pay for one of these new-fangled wireless sets, or some such.

In fact, I've been there myself. When I moved into my current house I decided, for some inexplicable reason, that it needed a different kitchen. The existing kitchen was already equipped with a cooker, some work surfaces, a sink and everything else essential to home motorcycle mainten-ance, but it was somehow a bit too floral and knotty for my liking.

And so – and I can hardly believe this now – I sold my Ducati 748 to a mate to pay for a new one. Obviously, he was not enough of a mate to take me to one side and point out that I was exchanging the evocative throb of the race-bred Italian V-twin for some prefabricated units. Oh no. He paid up, rode off and left me at the mercy of Poggenpohl and other oppressive regimes.

What was I thinking of? Did I think that when my motorcycling coevals came around of a Sunday I could fob them off with a shepherd's pie? Did I imagine that the relentless grinding of the Mouli Grater would be any sort of substitute for the gratifying tingle that the Ducati's engine produced at the base of my spine? And I'm not even married, so I can't blame what some of my correspondents have referred to as 'the management'.

Four years on I have acquired other motorcycles. But I have yet to produce anything pan-fried, oven-baked, seared or served on a bed of . . . Meanwhile, that same friend turns up almost every week on my old bike and blips the throttle outside the window to remind me that I am, in effect, about £5,000 down.

Men of all ages: put down this paper, rise up, and buy a motorcycle. Domesticity is for fools.

THE PEOPLE'S CRISP, PLUS A FAIRLY POPULAR CAR

I was in the pub the other day, I'd had a few, and obviously I needed a bag of crisps. 'Got any crisps?' I asked the bar bloke. 'Yes sir,' he replied. 'We've got roast beef and mustard, smoked ham and pickle, roast turkey and stuffing . . .'

I cut him short. 'Got any cheese and onion?'

He disappeared for a moment beneath the bar and then, without so much as a word of explanation, placed in front of me a bag of Brannigans cream cheese and chive flavoured oven-baked potato crisps. This was not what I wanted.

For a start, the flavour was completely wrong. They actually tasted of cream cheese and chives in bare-faced contravention of the ancient dictum that crisp flavours should bear no relation to those they are attempting to emulate. Blindfold me, place a Walker's beef crisp in my mouth and ask me to name the flavour and I would of course say 'beef'. But give me a real piece of beef with the same taste and I would immediately identify it as sun-dried cow pat. To experience the flavour of real cream cheese and chives together with the sensation of eating crisps is confusing to the educated pub-going palette.

Besides which, if there's one thing I can't stand, it's the intellectualisation of *pub fayre*. It makes my blood foam like a freshly pulled pint of Old Todger (og 1066). But my rage against this item from our selection of quality bar snacks (it said on the blackboard) was momentarily allayed on reading the packet. 'Van offer, only £3.99' it proclaimed above a picture of a small die-cast toy bearing the Brannigans logo. *The Model T Ford*, went the blurb, *is a classic vehicle which symbolises the dedication of Henry Ford in realising his vision of ownable transport for all.*

Now this was more to my taste. There has been a fashion, among revisionist historians and other people who ought to get a proper job, to portray my boyhood heroes – Edmund Hillary, Douglas Bader et al – not as topmost fellows but as utter rotters after all. I have recently read that Henry Ford was nothing but an ill-educated megalomaniac. But here was Brannigans telling it like it was: Ford was a swell guy who put the world's most car-conscious nation on wheels. It went on:

Mr Brannigan recognised that the Model T would provide him with the opportunity to deliver his delicious potato crisps to even more people and to realise his vision of quality crisps for all. Now this came as a surprise. I had long thought that the Model T was significant as the first, and hence most influential, of all true people's cars. Now, in the humble surroundings of my local, I learned that it was merely one element in the miracle of the people's crisp. It was all beginning to sound a bit half-baked. There was more:

Together these two pioneers have given everyone the chance to enjoy the delicious mouth-watering taste of Brannigans Thick Cut Potato Crisps. Now hang on. To use the nomenclature of the crisp business, this is 100 per cent tosh, piffle 'n' nonsense. In the pantheon of great thinkers I do not see a portrait of Henry Ford and his Model T – job number one from the world's car production line – next to one of Mr Brannigan holding an ancient snack recipe – unchanged since it was invented by a marketing man over lunch. In any case, Brannigan was not the great leveller his packaging would have you believe. The Model T was far cheaper than any car before it had ever been, but cheese and chive crisps cost a bloody fortune, as you'd expect of a product aimed at the bourgeois, the sort of people who buy Crunchy Nut Cornflakes because they have an innate desire, but class-ridden reluctance, to eat Frosties.

I would like to appeal to Brannigans to cease immediately this peddling of a fatuous marketing gimmick thinly disguised as a commemorative toy. The impact of the Model T is almost impossible to comprehend – consider that no maker of die-cast baubles, even at only £3.99 a shot, is likely to equal the real car's production run of well over twenty million units – and to assume equal billing with Henry Ford in the advancement of mankind's lot is conceited to say the least, even if you are the greatest philanthropist and social reformer the retail vegetable-based snack industry has yet produced.

Finally, I polished off the crisps. And do you know what? They tasted great. But I could have done without all the extra cheese.

Always read the packet.

KICKED IN THE NUTS BY A CAR MAKER

Be honest, do you *really* want to drive the Nissan Micra? Of course you don't. You may not know why you don't, or you may know but be loath to speak it. I shall say it for you: doe-eyed, comically rounded, nippy about town and incorrigibly cheeky, it is a girl's car.

Ooer, I hope you're ready to defend yourself, May. That's not exactly a *nineties* attitude is it? Hardly *egalitarian*, eh? No, it isn't, but then neither is Nissan's latest Micra ad. You must by now have seen it. I have to look at it almost every day, and every time I do I writhe in vicarious pain in my car seat. It's the one featuring that old 'ask before you borrow it' line and a close-up of some poor sod who's just been clobbered in the spuds by his woman. Sorry, *partner*.

Now, like many blokes, I'm a little unsure of the rules of engagement in the post-feminist society. But I do know this: if TVR came out with a poster showing a tearful young woman with a black eye and the line 'Cerbera – ask before you borrow it' there would be outrage. And so there should be about this Nissan ad. Men are angry. This one is anyway.

This poster – and notice how easily I slip into the vernacular of action groups, lobbyists and injured parties everywhere – is sending out the wrong message. Being thumped in the nads is never funny, not in a crappy TV comedy, an advert or – God forbid – real life. A man's plums are both the most vital part of his inheritance and source of the deposit he makes for posterity in the sacred vault of humankind's future. They are not, as my father used to say of double-barrelled shotguns, toys. I'm not suggesting for a moment that women's bits are any less important in all this, but we're not looking at a picture of a disembowelled woman, are we? If this poster is the work of 'men' in some horribly PC advertising agency then I can only assume that they aren't winning much business in the trouser department.

This advert – here we go again – portrays men as objects for abuse and trivialises their pods. If there is to be a battle of the sexes, then let it commence – it is an amusing facet of the human condition – but let's keep it above the belt. My feminist friends are fond of telling me that in the future men will be reduced to the status of mobile semen dispensers, which sounds great to me, but if they go around thinking it's OK to put the boot in where our tackle is concerned as well, then where will we be? Doubled up on the floor with no function, that's where.

In fact I've been worried by the decline in manhood for some time, what with recreational vehicles, bicycle racks, integral picnic tables and rumours of declining sperm counts. The Micra ad, and our pathetic tolerance of it, merely reinforces my suspicion that we're turning into a bunch of ruddy great jessies.

'You men are so ridiculously sensitive about them,' counters my younger sister. But what would she know? She can't possibly understand what it's like to be a man. I would like to make a formal call for the establishment of a pressure group to raise awareness . . . bollocks I would. I shall simply never buy the little Nissan, and I certainly don't want to borrow one after what I've seen. Neither should you, brothers. And girls – if you're hanging around with a bloke who keeps borrowing your Micra, may I suggest you dump him immediately? The man's obviously got no balls.

THE OLD OF TODAY – NO RESPECT FOR THEIR YOUNGERS

I like to think that you wouldn't know but I am now a staggering 33 years old. I am thus unwittingly contributing to one of the most acute problems facing our country – we are becoming ever more demographically challenged.

People are living longer, fewer babies are being born. It bodes ill for our industry and commerce, which will have an ever smaller pool of fresh and untainted minds on which to draw, though that may at least mean those minds will be afforded the opportunities they merit. It will mean a greater burden on the young for caring for the elderly, though that is a rightful and stabilising social duty. But these are trivial considerations compared with the obstacles our burgeoning old-fartedness threatens to place in the path of those young people embarking on the greatest and most accessible adventure the twentieth century has to offer – learning to drive.

I refer, of course, to the misguided campaign being pursued by old people everywhere to toughen up the driving test, quite the biggest red herring yet released into the pool of current motoring 'issues'. From the pages of the *RAC Magazine* to the letters column of *Daily Mirror Woman* one is assailed by thinly-disguised rants against youths' driving habits, all penned by people at least as old as me whose creaking, lumbering brains have grown too idle to recognise that the majority of road safety problems are merely the most apparent manifestation of deeper social ills affecting all ages.

These off-the-peg objections to young motorists fall to hand as readily as grandpa's story about not seeing a banana until he was 21; fortunately they are just as easily quashed. *A seventeen-year-old can pass the test and then go and drive a Ferrari.* Bloody good idea. A seventeen-year-old has the quick reactions and alert mind needed to deal with such things – you don't find old people on skateboards or flying combat aircraft. Clearly, speed belongs to the young. *Youngsters can pass the test one day and then drive on the motorway the next.* A good place to start – the cars are all going in the same direction, for Pete's sake. *Yes but young people are irresponsible.* You mean they have more accidents – but then they suffer more sports injuries and unwanted pregnancies, too. These are merely the legacy of youthful exuberance and are as inevitable as they are regrettable; they stem from an excess of enthusiasm, not a shortfall in skill. What difference would a tougher driving test make to that?

And so on. The truth is that it's convenient to blame the young and of course it's traditional; but whereas when I was a lad ancestral censure was merely an amusing facet of the human condition, my worry now is that the old are heading for majority rule and all that latent bitterness and twistedness will become an insuperable political force. Even the AA (91 this year) is displaying worrying signs. Recently, a spokesman announced that it was in favour of stricter testing, 'especially for young people who don't have the experience of older drivers'. Well, in my experience, experience counts for nought: experience is as likely to take the form of the bloke who nearly knocked me off my bike the other day, who probably saw a MkI Cortina last time he looked in the mirror and who was no doubt busy telling his wife how he ' 'ant 'ad an accident in fotty year'. The AA is an excellent organisation but they forget that they were young once.

So – young people are obviously better equipped, both mentally and physically, for driving; older people can boast length of service, but that can't be relied upon to confer any benefit. Therefore, our new test should be applied to all *current* road users, too. That should see enthusiasm for the project wane. It should dwindle to nothing when it is realised that this will mean taking the proposed written exam, and that people who haven't read the highway code since it had stuff about traction engines in it will be required to remember the appropriate uses of the horn and the function of the inside lane on the M1. Still keen? Try my Part 1 test before campaigning further.

1 **Which of the following should you have in your car?**

   (a) A brown hat.
   (b) A hardback road atlas.
   (c) *Now That's What I Call Music* vol. 36.

2 **Where should the tax disc be displayed?**

   (a) In the lower left-hand corner of the windscreen.
   (b) In a polished chrome surround attached to the radiator grille.
   (c) In the post.

3 **How long have you been driving?**

   (a) I learned in an Austin A40 – wonderful car.
   (b) Fotty year.
   (c) It's insured in my dad's name.

4 **What is the fundamental rule of the road?**

   (a) Keep left.
   (b) Keep forgetting to signal.
   (c) Keep a box of tissues on the rear parcel shelf.

5 **Which of the following most affects forward visibility?**

   (a) Bi-focals.
   (b) Traffic film.
   (c) The top of the steering wheel.

6 Which of the following should you check before a long journey?

(a) That the tyres are inflated to the correct pressure for sustained high-speed driving.

(b) The thermos flask fluid level.

(c) That you have been to the lavatory.

How did you score?

6 a=30, b=20, c=10
1 a=10, b=20, c=30 2 a=20, b=10, c=30 3 a=20, b=30, c=10 4 a=30, b=20, c=10 5 a=10, b=20, c=30

141–180 You are fit to drive.

101-140 You should consider the campaign for better public transport.

60-100 Pull over when safe to do so and continue on foot, if able.

GERMANY INVADES – RING CHURCH BELLS AND PUT THE KETTLE ON

A few weeks ago I was very worried about the Germans and by last Friday afternoon I was even more worried. The Germans, as five minutes with any GCSE history book will reveal, want to take over our country and these days are attempting it with a stealthy invasion of our beleaguered motor industry. Faced with a Home Guard armed with nothing more than a few sticks of walnut and an old radiator grille, they appear unstoppable.

Yet by Sunday evening I realised that Britain would never, ever be subjugated by Jerry. Never. So now we can relax.

But before I could feel better about the whole business I had to feel worse. And I felt very bad on Friday afternoon when a man appeared at my door to deliver my smoke for the weekend, a Mercedes-Benz CL600. Here, I sensed within minutes of driving away, was one of the finest motor cars I had ever driven. Not only does the CL look utterly fantastic, it also goes like hell, courtesy of its 6.0-litre V12.

At the same time it is calming, dignified and supremely comfortable. It is also so comprehensively equipped that the owner's handbook leaves no space even for a pair of fingerless mittens in that compartment we insist on calling the 'glove box'. Even the satellite navigation system seemed to work properly, though at one point the icy fraulein instructed me to 'prepare to carry straight on ahead'.

It is the undisputed obergruppenführer of all cars. In one decisive überholvorgang (ie overtaking manoeuvre) it has put everything I thought I knew about posh motors into rapidly diminishing perspective. Abso-bloody-lutely su-bloody-perb mate.

It is, of course, only a car. Or is it? To my mind there are three things that tell you everything you need to know about any given nation: the state of its lavatories, the efficiency of its national airline, and the quality of the cars it produces. Germany scores well in all three and of these, the car is the most important. The motor industry is the front line of the new global battlefield and any country that can produce the CL600 is going to come storming over the top and stick a giant technological and corporate bayonet in everyone else's guts.

But they still won't win in the end and I shall now tell you why. On Saturday, my house guest for the weekend arrived, a German friend of many years standing who rejoices in the faintly Teutonic name of Armin Helmut Göbelbecker. No sooner had Goebbels' gigantic jack boots stepped onto the doormat than he said, as he always does, 'Chames, please, I would now like a cup of great British tea'.

And so I made him one, and it tasted great. He then made me one, and it tasted like something a schweinhund had done in the teapot.

I have known this bloke since I was twelve, and every time I see him I go through the motions of instructing him how to make tea properly. I have made gifts to him of teapots and boxes of the finest British tea blends, and I may as well have given them to the beasts in the fields. What he produces with them amounts to pure filth. I have even made the tea myself only to have him pour it out, and the delicate process of infusion is somehow corrupted by the proximity of his Germanness. He cannot, and will never be able to, make a decent cup of Rosie.

Yes, yes, I know. Pompous English bloke complains about foreigners' inability to produce a decent cuppa. It's crucial to the world order. Tea is without question what made this country great. There is a theory that says the industrial revolution started here because the medicinal effects of widespread tea drinking kept our emerging industrial cities free of bowel disorders and allowed them to flourish. I can believe it. Continentals were all drinking double espressos and were far too jittery and hyperactive to sit down and invent the steam engine.

The Germans will achieve so much in Britain but then, in accordance with historical precedent, they will push us a bit too far and we'll then be forced to send them away with a bloody nose. This point will come when they enter the kitchen and put the kettle on.

The Germans make terrific cars but, like all foreigners, they are ultimately undone because they can't make a proper pot of char. In the Italians, this failing is charming conceit. In the French it is arrogance. But in the Germans, it is the destruction of the myth of their supremacy and very reassuring as a result.

I am now going to ring up and ponce a Bentley. Hang on – they're German, aren't they?

CHARITY BEGINS IN THE CAR

Two pieces of junk mail and a car launch hardly sound like a starting point for a solution to world poverty, but life-saving initiatives have had shakier starts than that. The man who invented Catseyes, one Percy Shaw, was inspired when he came out of the pub pissed one night and used the moonlight reflecting off the tram lines to guide him home. And he has undoubtedly saved lives over the years.

First came a press release from Drive & Survive, purveyors of training courses to the nation's company car drivers, entitled 'Fatal Distraction'. It goes on to say, somewhat unequivocally, that 'lack of concentration can have a huge impact on the chance of a collision', before listing some of the in-car diversions that can be a driver's undoing – mobile phones, fags, brats in the back and so on. But they left out a significant one.

Now to the launch of the new Ford Mondeo, a very fine car with a simply mind-blowing cup holder. The Mondeo is refined and quiet, it handles predictably but pleasingly, and the suspension set-up is one of the best I've encountered for some time. Yet all Ford's efforts in these areas appear as mere tinkerings in a shed compared with the sheer wit and ingenuity that has been discharged in the design of its cup holder.

Press the flush-mounted plastic rectangle on the facia and the holder extends with perfectly choreographed precision into a sort of plastic balletic first position. It really needs a quick burst of Prokofiev on the sound system to complete the illusion. I was so entranced by it that I very nearly drove into a wall.

This is not the first time a cup holder has nearly killed me. The first time was at the launch of the Saab 9-5. Nestling within the wood-effect dash, which is actually real wood, is a slim vertical strip of something that looks rather less like plastic. Press this – and you will press it, in the same way that you'll always try a tea cosy on your head – and it tilts, pivots and rotates to proffer a cup holder in the way a butler might proffer your post on a silver tray.

There's a lot of this sort of nonsense about. Mercedes-Benz has a cup holder that bursts forth from the dash like a time-lapse film of a daffodil opening. Toyota has one that matches the complexity of an aeroplane's landing gear and which, though nominally a cup holder, is actually presented as an on-board celebration of the lifetime's work of Euclid. The amount of research and development time expended on this thing would once, not so long ago, have sufficed for a whole new car.

You probably think the world's motor industry is competing in terms of price, customer service, standard equipment, warranties and all the rest of the stuff that matters to the average owner. It is not. It is embroiled in a bitter contest to see who can produce the most ludicrous cup holder.

Open a car brochure these days and there will almost certainly be a perfectly lit photograph of a Maxpax hot chocolate with a soft-focus car interior receding into the background. I have been at press presentations on car launches where grown men with wives and family responsibilities have stood up and given forth on the damping mechanism of the new car's cup holder. I came away from the launch of the Nissan Almera knowing all about this but unable to remember what sort of engine it had.

And it has got to stop. Because, in the end, cup holders are just somewhere to put a cup, and no one that I associate with actually takes afternoon tea in the car anyway. The amount of time and creative energy expended on the cup-holder race could probably be used to rid the world of all known diseases.

Which brings me to my second item of junk mail, a humbling appeal from the director of Oxfam for a dona-

tion of £2 a month to help the world's poor. Two quid –
now I think of it, that's barely enough to buy a couple of
plastic cups of horrible coffee from a motorway service
station.

But I'm not going to give them £2 a month. Instead, every
time I encounter a cup holder in a new car, I'm going to
donate, on behalf of the motor industry, a fiver to Oxfam's
project to dig fresh-water wells in Sudan.

The cup holder is beginning to look remarkably like a
monument to the developed world's decadence, especially
when you remember that we inherited the idea from the
Americans, who wouldn't buy Jaguars until the company
came up with somewhere for them to put their Coke. And
that's McDonald's cola, sir.

Meanwhile, there are people in Africa who are dying for
a drink.

CYCLE YOUR WAY TO ARMAGEDDON

The cycling lobby, I am delighted to be able to announce, has got it all wrong. Bicycles are not, after all, a universal panacea to the congestive disorders afflicting the world's cities – they are the cause of it. Who'd have thought it?

Before the bicycle, normal people didn't really go anywhere. As the bicycle developed, people were able to stray further from their homes to the extent that by the turn of the nineteenth century, a whole social phenomenon had developed in the form of the cycle tour. You can see it celebrated on old posters and engravings reproduced on the lids of biscuit barrels.

So far so good. The bicycle was, after all, a great invention; it liberated the common people immeasurably and was fuelled by nothing more than the then equivalent of a Mars Bar. Unfortunately, it also generated an insatiable taste for personal mobility, and the desire to go further, faster, eventually led to the invention of the motor car. Now the world is full of them, and where once Victorian man might have walked downstairs to toil at the forge, his descendants might now drive fifty miles to work in an advertising agency.

If it hadn't been for the bicycle, none of this would have happened.

It is probably safe to say that every time a bicycle frame is brazed together, the desire for a car is created somewhere. Think back to your childhood. You rode your first tricycle around the garden. Your first proper bicycle was probably ridden up and down the road. As you matured you owned bigger and better bikes, rode further afield, fitted a horn, built a scrambler, experimented with centre-pull brakes and generally exhausted the potential of the thing until, at the age of seventeen, you were foaming at the mouth and ready to chuck the bike in the shed and borrow your dad's car.

We can never overestimate the impact that the bicycle business has had on the fabric of the world. Last week, I was in the Czech Republic visiting the home of Lauren & Klement, the business partnership that was to become Skoda. Klement was a harmless bookseller, but Laurin was a mechanic. Together, in 1895, they decided to build bicycles. Within a few years they were fitting engines to them and just ten years later, they had built their first car. The bicycle can therefore be blamed for the Skoda Rapid coupé if nothing else.

And the Skoda story is not a unique one. The Rover car business was founded with something called, rather confusingly, the Rover Safety Bicycle. Developments in, among other things, chain and sprocket technology had allowed Rover to create a genuinely practical machine that could be ridden and maintained with ease by just about anyone. Bearded historians of the bicycle rightly hold it up as a quantum leap in the machine's evolution but fail to recognise that, in taking the bicycle forward, Rover merely brought the car closer.

Honda Soichiro, you may remember, established his automotive empire by buggering about with bicycle components. Fiat made bicycles, and Peugeot still does. In 1903, a pair of bored bicycle builders gave us the aeroplane.

There is obviously something deeply fatuous about rich bankers and scruffy media types riding around on bicycles on the grounds of morality. Let's face it – you don't ride a bicycle for ethical reasons, you ride one because you're poor. Postie has a bicycle, but not because it's good for him or the planet – it's because the Post Office is too tight to buy him a van.

Gandhi may have walked everywhere, but a large proportion of India's people will currently be found on the saddle of a bike. The Indians seem to have a great affection for the humble bicycle and regard each and every one as a family heirloom. But as India's trade barriers come down and its economy is reinvigorated, this affection will be eclipsed by a perfectly natural urge to move up to a car. You will not sell a politically correct titanium mountain bike to a bloke who, for a few thousand quid, can have a Maruti 800. So there's another billion potential car-sales leads generated by this subversive but largely ignored cult of pedalling.

I've never been to China but I've seen enough pictures of the place to know that it is the world epicentre of bicycling. There are so many bicycles on the roads of China that if you fell off one in Beijing the resulting mass swerving of cyclists taking evasive action would cause an inadvertent bicycle-mounted Chinese invasion of the surrounding countries.

News reaches me today from a business journalist of my acquaintance that China is consolidating its 120-plus minor car assembly plants and lobbying to join the World Trade Organisation. Numerous Western car makers have been sniffing around China for years in anticipation of this. Why? Because they know that every one of those bicycles has the potential to metamorphose into a car. There are campaigners in the West claiming that this scenario spells disaster, but why shouldn't the Chinese have cars? I've got one.

And to think that there are people pedalling past your window, even as you read this, in the belief that they're doing the decent thing. If you are one of them, and you honestly believe that the car is tearing decent society apart and destroying the planet, I'll tell you what you should do – kill your bicycle.

NOT DROWNING BUT DRIVING

This week, I've come over all charitable and decided to do something to help the lifeboats.

The reason is fairly simple – whilst enjoying a pleasant pub-crawl along the banks of the Thames the other evening, I saw the inland arm of the RNLI successfully rescue a woman who had fallen into the river and was in danger, as Tennyson would have put it, of crossing the bar.

Using an impressive rigid inflatable boat and a very powerful torch, they located the hapless, floundering damsel, wrapped her in big blankets and brought her ashore. 'No one's drowning in my river,' said our sou'westered hero, sternly, in an impromptu post-rescue interview with a slightly blotto bloke from the *Daily Telegraph*.

To be honest, I had no idea that the RNLI operated on the Thames, but they've been doing just that since 2001 in response to the *Marchioness* disaster. It transpires, in fact, that the Tower Pier boathouse is the busiest in the whole business. Last year it was scrambled (or whatever it's called in lifeboating) on average once a day, and saved 134 souls who might otherwise be bobbing against the Thames Barrier. And this is just a charity.

It's very relevant, too. My mum and dad are boatists, I have a small inflatable that I use on the Thames and, of course, I spend a great deal of time wandering amongst the bankside taverns of a river that even Samuel Pepys identified as a significant cause of sudden and unexpected death in the capital. The RNLI is an invaluable service to those in peril coming out of the pub and therefore, in accordance with my Rules of Donation, deserves a tenner.

Then again, £10 doesn't buy very much. The RNLI costs £300,000 a day to run, so even the five minutes they're going to need to pluck me out of the drink is going to cost £1000. That's how much I need to put in the tin and there's the problem, because that means organising a sponsored charity fund-raising event.

I'm a bit uneasy about these things. The London Marathon is great, because it involves a genuine human achievement that I couldn't manage. The British Heart Foundation is a worthy cause so if any of my mates are entering the marathon, I'll sponsor them.

But it can get silly. A children's hospice is a worthy cause too, so they can have a tenner. They can have it straight away. I don't need to see someone sit naked in a bathtub of cold baked beans for twelve hours before releasing the cash.

Let's say the local maternity unit needs some extra cash for equipment. They can have £10. In fact, they can have £20 if they promise that no grown men will dress up in nappies and push an old hospital bed through the local shopping centre.

Up at the BBC, to take a real-life example, a couple of people are seeking sponsorship for riding recumbent bicycles from London to Sydney in aid of Cancer Research and Children in Need. They can have a tenner anyway. I don't need to witness an adventure-cum-achievement first. Apart from anything else, I don't think they'll make it on recumbent bicycles. They'll be knocked off within a few miles by a van driver who hasn't seen them. Serves them right. No one likes a smart-arse.

But back to the lifeboats – I want to raise £1,000, as I have a sort of vested interest, and I've decided that the best and most efficient way of doing this is with a sponsored drive from Land's End to John o' Groats.

I know what you're thinking: that's not much of an achievement. And you'd be right. It's even less of an achievement than you think, because I intend to take two days over the journey and stop at a nice hotel. What's more, I'm going to do it in something like a Bentley or a Ferrari, which I'm going to blag from the appropriate manufacturer by ringing up and blackmailing them with an 'it's for charity' approach.

But that's not the point. The point is that the RNLI needs cash to continue its vital work, and it needs the money now. I have to raise the cash as quickly as possible. The recumbent cyclists are going to take a year to raise £50,000 and that's far too long. People could drown while I'm pedalling pointlessly instead of taking the car.

Below is the sponsorship form. Please give what you can – a pound will do. As soon as you've pledged the £1,000, I'll be off.

NEVER RACED OR RALLIED, NO FAMOUS OWNERS. GOOD.

You may not know this, but during the First World War a certain German corporal called Adolf Hitler narrowly avoided being shot.

If I remember it rightly – I can't actually be bothered to look it up – he was awarded a medal for gallantry after he rescued a wounded comrade from no-man's land. It was during this incident that some unknown British or French foot-slogger, had he had the benefit of great foresight, or even a correctly adjusted one, would come to wish he'd spent more time practising at the butts. With Adolf taken out by a .303 round, the world would now be a very different place.

This brings me neatly – bear with me on this – to *Top Gear*'s Restoration Rip-Off feature, as seen on TV in the last series. In case you weren't watching, we had five broken cars of historic significance, all in need of extensive repair, and we could afford to restore one of them. You decided which one in a telephone vote. If you think we got the idea from that programme about old buildings, you'd be right.

There was a Lotus that had been ordered by James Dean, but which he never saw because he died soon afterwards; the Probe 16 used in *A Clockwork Orange*; a Chrysler Wimbledon once driven into a duck pond by Who drummer Keith Moon; a Range Rover used by Chas and Di on their honeymoon; and a Mini Cooper driven by Paddy Hopkirk in the Monte Carlo Rally. In the end, the Hopkirk Cooper, although it failed to win in the white heat of competition during the early 60s, romped home to a decisive victory while it was merely disintegrating in some bloke's shed, beating the second-placed spares-or-repair case by a margin of two to one.

Thank you for taking the trouble to vote, and may I say well done. To be honest, I wanted the Moon Chrysler to win, because I thought it the most interesting car, it was the one I most wanted to drive, and it was easily the most original and unmolested of the five. I actually thought the Range Rover would cream it, because British sentimentality would triumph over concerns for our motoring heritage and people would press four on their touch-tone phones in a 10p electronic tribute to the dear departed Queen of Hearts. Either that or the James Dean Lotus would be seen as a suitable memorial to a man whose other car is probably beyond economic repair. But no – the Mini victory suggests that, in the end, you're still more interested in cars than in celebrity. And so, as it happens, am I.

I've been thinking about this business of provenance and what a lot of nonsense it all is. By way of illustration, I said something really quite fatuous in the film about the Dean Lotus. This was a car the screen legend ordered but grew tired of waiting for, and the Porsche he bought to be going on with was the car that killed him. 'What if this Lotus had been delivered on time?' I asked. 'Maybe James Dean would still be alive.'

Well, that's quite possibly true, but now I think about it a bit harder I realise that it is also complete nonsense. Going back to Hitler, let's imagine he had been shot in the trenches. People in pubs wouldn't be saying 'Hey, it's a good job that bloke with the funny 'tache got shot, otherwise Poland would have been invaded and Europe would have been divided by an iron curtain for a generation.' Likewise, if the Lotus had turned up on time I wouldn't have ended up making a film about a knackered Porsche 356 Speedster and claiming it was the car that could have killed James Dean, while showing archive pictures of him driving around happily in his Lotus. The world is full of cars that haven't killed famous people. There are numerous Cadillacs out there that were once owned by Elvis Presley, and he died taking a dump.

If provenance is important, then celebrity provenance is the sort you don't want. So the Chrysler was owned by Keith Moon. This is hardly encouraging. Did you see what he did to his drum kit? And his hotel room? And himself, for that matter. Why would I want the ex royal wedding Range Rover? The Royal Family didn't think it was that significant, otherwise it wouldn't be rotting away in a barn.

The dealer ads in classic car magazines are full of this sort of thing. A Bentley or similar is advertised as being 'ex Greta Garbo' or whatever. If it still had Greta Garbo in it, or even just smelled of her, then I might be interested. Otherwise, I don't see how it's going to improve the car in any way. Likewise a Duesenberg that was once owned by Errol Flynn. It's not the sort of service history that bodes well for the condition of the car.

'Former titled owner' is another one seen on the odd ad for an old Roller or Bristol. Personally, I'd keep quiet about this. Take a look at the state of the average toff's house and it becomes immediately clear that you shouldn't buy a second-hand car from this bloke.

In any case, what difference will it actually make to the experience of driving? Jeremy Clarkson, for example, is officially titled, being Dr Jeremy Clarkson (but please don't go to him with any medical ailments, because his is an honorary doctorate from a technical university. Whatever you've got he'll have had first, and much bigger).

I still don't want his old car. I wouldn't drive along suffused by a warm inner glow generated by the knowledge that this was once Dr Clarkson's car. I'd be driving along picking nub ends out of the upholstery and wondering why every button on the radio gives me Terry Wogan.

I accept that I'm a bloke who once asked what the 'L' in L MacPherson stands for, and which F1 team he was in, but even so, I find the whole celebrity motoring thing a bit creepy. And it doesn't stop with old stuff. Note how pleased manufacturers are when an England footballer buys their Ferrari or Porsche or Mercedes-Benz. Is this supposed to recommend it to me? Am I to think I will enjoy the sexual allure of David Beckham and co. if I go out and buy the same thing? If anything, it puts me off.

I mean, our boys haven't scored in ages.

QUESTIONS OF STYLE

GERMANS VICTORIOUS IN WORLD COUPE FINAL

I don't know. Perhaps it was the devastation of last month's World Cup defeat, or perhaps I'm genuinely growing up, but whatever it is, I seem to be mellowing rapidly. A month ago, fuelled by France '98 fervour, I was an angst-ridden youth vigorously defending for England against Germany in the wake of the Rolls buy-out by VW. This month I think Jerry is a splendid fellow. I've even found a BMW I like.

I've always accepted that BMWs are good cars; square-jawed, Teutonic, smelling faintly of Bratwurst and all that *Victor Annual* stuff, but they've never really been my kind of thing. I've always preferred the austerity and understatement of a Mercedes-Benz. BMWs are a bit overtly sporting for my torpid liking. As a TV presenter might say, if this BMW were a German, it would be Jurgen Klinsmann. But a Mercedes is some white-haired boffin working away quietly on his heavy water project.

The car that has changed my mind is the most unlikely in the BM line-up. It is the Z coupé, the . . . well, what it is exactly I don't know.

I first saw this car ages ago, at some motor show or other. I was gambolling gaily across the exhibition hall in unerring pursuit of some incisive nugget of investigative journalism – going to sit in an Aston Martin, probably – when something hideous registered in my peripheral vision. It was so ugly I thought it must be just some fatuous upstart plastic supercar, but as I swivelled my head I realised it was the much anticipated BMW Z coupé. What an abomination. *Dummkopfs*, I thought, without even breaking my step.

That was the last I thought of it until, last week, an invitation to drive the thing plopped into that space where, in a proper household, the doormat would be. As we arrived at the hotel in Munich, there it was again, right outside reception on a raised plinth. I have to say I still didn't like it. 'Looks as though it was styled by Marcos,' I said during pre-dinner drinks to the BMW GB man, who simply walked away and left me at the mercy of a bunch of Germans. 'So,' said one – when Germans speak English they always begin with 'so' – 'what do you think of the coupé, *ja*?'

This was a delicate issue, so I thought it best to reply in the native tongue. Now school German, at least up to the age where you fail to qualify for the O-level rounds, is not exactly everyday conversational stuff. I have visited Germany many times – I even have a god-daughter there – but I have never once had an opportunity to proclaim *Aber ja, natürlich Hans ist nass, er steht unter dem Wasserfall* (why, of course Hans is wet, he's standing under the waterfall). It just doesn't happen. I have booked countless wake-up calls at German hotel receptions in the hope of being able to concur that *wenn der Wecker läutet, steht Mann auf* (when the alarm clock rings, one gets up) but, to be honest, the opportunity has never arisen. *Die Katze springt auf und das Spiegelei fällt auf dem Boden* (the cat leaps up and the fried egg falls on the floor) – no, not that one either.

Then I remembered the episode in the school text book *Sprich Mal Deutsch* (speak crap German, presumably) where Hans goes into the dark shed looking for his bicycle pump and finds a big spider – *Die Spinne ist hässlich* (the spider is hideous). '*Hässlich*,' I cried triumphantly. He smiled fondly and changed the subject to the World Cup. '*Scheisse*,' I opined, as we'd already been knocked out and Germany was to play Croatia that evening. 'Your German is good,' said this awfully civilised Bavarian. 'It's this *Weissbier*,' I replied, raising my glass. 'A few more of these and I'll think your coupé looks pretty good as well.' Fortunately, there was then a call to the corporate barbecue and we all tramped outside to eat schnitzel.

The wurst was yet to come, I'd polished off another couple of *grosse biers* and the place was crawling with Germans wanting to ask my opinion of the Z coupé. So, fearful of ending up on the front page of the *Sun* as the man who disgraced England, I wandered into the garden to look at the car again. It really was suffering a crisis of identity somewhere around the B pillar, as if the designers of the two ends had met there and agreed to disagree. A German was lurking at 12 o'clock, so I chose discretion and retreated to bed.

The next day I drove it. Well. The 2.8-litre Z coupé is, in all honesty, the better car, but the M-power version, the only one we're getting, is the one I want. I'd been looking at it wrongly. Once I'd stopped seeing a roadster that had undergone conversion to a hearse and recognised instead a practical hatchback with a supercar nose grafted on I had to acknowledge that I'd been comprehensively outflanked by the German sense of humour. Here was a grand tourer in the best tradition, and once the fog of my hangover had cleared, the continent no longer seemed cut off.

That evening, back in dear old Blighty, I went to the pub to watch Germany vs Croatia on the telly and, for the first time in my life, found myself rooting for the old enemy. But they lost three–nil. Still, as somebody somewhere no doubt said, it was a victory for football. And the BMW Z coupé is a car of two halves.

CAR ACCESSORIES – THEY'RE A CRIME IN THEMSELVES

The other day, I was driving along in my old Mini when the gearknob came off in my hand.

You know how it goes: a snappy change down to third on a tight left-hander during a rare moment of sporty driving, and my clenched fist, still gripping the plastic ball, simply continued on its way until it made bone-crunching contact with the cast-off BL switches on the facia.

Fortunately, though, it wasn't the first time this had happened to me. Back in my youth I had another Mini, and the gearknob came off that one as well. So I knew what was required: all I had to do was stop at one of those countless high-street car-spares shops called something like *Top Gear*, ask for a new gearknob for a Mini, and pay a few quid for a piece of tat in a Unipart box. Screw it on to the threaded end of the gear stick, and I'd be on my way.

Well. In the first shop, I had some difficulty convincing the fickle youth behind the counter that there had been another Mini before the one he knew about, and that it was a cheap car on which no small spare should ever cost more than a fiver. So the manager stepped in.

'I'd like a gearknob for an old Mini,' I explained. So he led me, while extracting a huge bunch of keys from his pocket, to a triple-locked glass display cabinet of the sort used to display ancient manuscripts in the British Museum.

There were leather gearknobs, suede gearknobs, two-tone gearknobs, a silver gearknob with an enamelled naked woman on it, and a contoured gearknob for extra gearshift pleasure. One of them cost over £60. I began to wonder if he kept the really hard-core gearknobs behind the counter.

'It's just an old Mini,' I explained. 'I'd like something simple, and plastic.'

So he led me to a lesser cabinet with only one lock, and showed me a gearknob shaped like the grip of a Schmieser machine pistol. It was truly preposterous. This man really couldn't understand that I just wanted something that enabled me to change gear without sustaining an injury from the threaded end of the stick. To him, the knob was at the core of the enthusiastic motorist's being.

Obviously, I didn't buy anything, for fear that my Mini would look like a gearknob with an aftermarket car fitted. And since that day I have been driving around with a bleeding left hand determined to find the £3 knob of my youth.

But all I have discovered is that there are whole communities out there being supported by people doing dreadful things to cars. And gearknobs are just the beginning.

Obviously, I am familiar with the alloy wheel craze currently sweeping the nation. I accept, also, that what I know about being cool could be written on the label in my cardigan. But I still wasn't quite prepared for the scene that would greet me at the wheel depot where I met my colleague Richard Hammond and his new Dodge Charger.

There were people here with quite ordinary machinery buying wheels at a price that I still think of as the budget for a whole car. There were three-spoke, five-spoke, dished, flat, chromed and split-rim wheels going on to humdrum Fiestas and old Hondas. Builders were turning up to fit £1,500-worth of wheels to panel vans. Where they find the money I don't know, since none of them ever turn up for work.

And then there was Hammond's Charger. Personally, I rather liked the original pressed-steel wheels for their comedy value. Here is a car with over seven litres of V8 but with pathetic little wheels inset like the ones on a Commer camper van. It would have been fun watching them disintegrate, especially as Hamster has had the lump up-rated to give the same torque as a diesel shunter.

But no. He wanted some phat alloys: 21 inches and chromed at that. While the car was up in the air having them fitted I seriously considered having a quick shave. Needless to say, the list price for these things is not far off what I paid for an entire Range Rover.

But it could be worse, because he could go for this so-called privacy glass next. This stuff really baffles me. What sort of person honestly needs privacy in a car? Not anyone genuinely famous, I'd wager. The other day, driving down a dual carriageway, I was overtaken by no less a comic luminary than Rowan Atkinson driving a McLaren F1. He's the sort of person we might want to look at, and yet the glass in his car appeared to be the same as the stuff in the window of my office.

Similarly, we had two of Nick Mason's Ferraris on the show the other day, and they were both fitted with normal see-through glass allowing us to view the ageing rock legend and author in complete clarity. And then there's the Queen, quite probably the most famous woman in the world. She's actually had a car built with extra glass, so we can see her even better as she makes her way to the hat shop.

I can only conclude that people fit smoked glass so I can't see just how unremarkable they are; so I can't go into the pub and say 'Hey, you'll never guess who I saw driving a 5-series BMW today. A normal bloke.'

It would be harmless enough if it didn't cause such problems on the roads. Near my house, for example, there is a complex junction fed by three separate roads that demands considerable skill to negotiate safely. As I sweep through it on my way to the *Top Gear* office, there's a good chance I'll meet someone else vying for a place on the same four-lane stretch that the three feeder roads join.

Obviously, I indicate. But it's not enough. In that yawning instant when the two cars come together, I need to be able to look the other bloke in the eye, so we can converse with those subtle nods and inclinations of the head that mean 'after you' or 'hang on mate, I'm just moving left a bit'. But of course, he's driving a 4 × 4 with big alloys and privacy glass, and for all I know he could be doing the crossword.

Still, let's look on the bright side. At least I can't see his knob.

THE MAZDA MX-5, AN EQUAL OPPORTUNITIES SPORTS CAR

There was a time, around the time that Enid Blyton was at her most prolific, when I could reasonably have described my MX-5 as gay. According to Chambers Dictionary, which I have borrowed from the library, that would make it 'lively, bright, sportive, merry', which sounds about right. But of course I'm not to say it now, because it would be taken as a cheap dig at my brethren on the other bus. And I do not want that, for I believe that whatever a bloke does with his old man is his own business.

Anyway. The bloke I met on the pavement the other day, as I parked up, had no such qualms. He said the MX-5 was a hairdresser's car and that I must be a 'kin poofter.

I'm getting a bit fed up with this. There are two types of people in the world and they occupy both sexes: those who think the MX-5 is great, and those who think it is an unequivocal testimony to my mother's original desire for a girl or something. I'm completely familiar with the trite theories that motor cars are an unwitting statement about the swordsmanship of their owners, but the notion that my car is gay is nothing more than the transparent rantings of an inadequate in the trousorial arena. Consider this: if I were to pull up in something ostensibly macho – a TVR for example – would I be accosted by gay men accusing me of sexual congress with women? I don't think so, but I'll have to try it around Soho one evening. I'll get back to you on this one.

And what, exactly, is a 'hairdresser's car'? Clearly, this is a deeply sensitive issue that discerning people would not raise over dinner. But this is an incisive magazine that does not balk at addressing the socio-political nuances with which the world of motoring is riddled, and I have been conducting some thorough research.

It's about time the mug shot at the top of my column was updated, because I've had so many haircuts in the last two months, to this end, that I've hardly got any left. The impression to my closest friends is that my hair is growing backwards. The long and short of my tireless work is this.

Gary, of Dazzle Hair and Beauty, who took the rug you see above to the Stephen Fry stage, has a Vauxhall Vectra with a roof-box. Style-wise, this is a bald bloke who grows it long on one side and slaps it over the top with Brylcreem. Gary doesn't have much hair, as it happens. His choice of wheels tells me little about which camp he's in, so I have to conclude that he's just a bloke who cuts hair.

Hard on his heels, and reducing the mop-top to a simple tufted rug, is Keith of Keith's Men's Modern Hairstyles, who drives a Hyundai Snarter which, in the car-hairstyle analogy, is a 70s footballer's perm and a bit long at the back at that. Curiously, Keith himself sports just such a barnet, so one can only assume he hasn't scored for either side in ages.

John, of John's Gentlemen's Hairdressers, a sort of contraceptive outlet that does a discreet sideline in haircuts, tidied up the square-headed U-boat commander's cut I got on the VW Lupo launch before revealing that he drives an old Sierra. What does this tell me? It tells me that John has fallen on hard times. The man can't even afford a bottle of shampoo – his long hair looks like Aphrodite's would if she'd come ashore where the Amoco Cadiz went aground. Clearly, his barber's pole isn't drawing in the punters either way.

In fact, I have yet to meet a hairdresser of either sex who drives an MX-5 or, for that matter, an Escort Cabrio. There is *no such thing* as a hairdresser's car. Good. Now what about a gay one?

Bill, of Bill's Clip Joint, brought me to my current tonsorial status with a number three buzz up the back and sides. The Mazda was parked right outside. 'Do you think my car is gay?' I asked him. 'Well, sir,' he said, 'You seem very happy with it.'

A queer fellow and no mistake.

I AM NOT AN EXECUTIVE, I AM A FREE MAN

A word that has always bothered me is 'gala'. I've been to gala dinners, gala breakfasts, gala awards ceremonies and gala opening nights, but I've never been able to discern exactly what attribute separates these events from any other dinner, breakfast, ceremony or night.

I'm beginning to think that 'gala' is just a meaningless word used in an attempt to dignify tiresome social events involving eats on sticks, rather in the way that local government officials, when interviewed on the radio about burglary or drugs, always rely on 'in the community' to lend themselves extra gravitas.

Still, no one to my knowledge has yet launched a gala car, although Isuzu, makers of the Trooper Citation, may be thinking about it.

'Executive' is another word that has me worried and is a different matter altogether, because we do have the 'executive car'. Now: I'm happy with the idea of a people-carrier, an off-roader or an estate, because I know what distinguishes them. People carriers carry more people than a regular car, off-roaders are engineered and built to be driven off road by bankers' wives and gay interior designers, and estates carry more marvellous antique chairs that you bought from a wonderful little shop in Islington than you can fit in a normal four-door saloon. But what makes a car 'executive'? I haven't yet come across one with a built-in secretary or overhead PowerPoint presentation projector.

Come to think of it, what is an executive anyway? I know lots of them, many of them old friends whose ascent of the executive ladder I have charted since we left school together. But I still don't know what they do for a living. All I know is that they carry expensive manbags packed with laptops, Palm Pilots and other personal electronic business machines that have to be 'upgraded' every few months. On that basis, an executive car is one with room for a briefcase on board, which admits pretty much everything this side of Formula One.

So 'executive car' is beginning to look like a way of saying 'car', rather in the way that 'manufacturing facility' turns out to mean 'factory'. It's another bit of business babble. That's sorted then.

Or is it? The trouble is that although I am at a loss to define the executive car, I recognise that some have an undeniable executive quality. It starts, at the top – where it's tough, apparently – with the Maybach 62. Ostensibly, this is a luxury car, but after a few hours on board you realise that it is, in fact, another management tool. It doesn't matter what mood you're in when you climb in to the reclining back seat; by the time you step out again you're ready to oversee the merger of two European petrochemical giants.

Lower down the corporate command chain, the Vauxhall Vectra offers a similar experience. Whenever I drive one – whether it be on a motorway, a winding B-road, along the coast or simply to a supermarket – I can never quite shake off the nagging impression that I'm en route to a conference on the future of injection moulding in the plastics industry.

I'm convinced that this isn't simply a matter of preconception. The Rolls-Royce Phantom, though a Maybach rival on paper, is not in any way executive. It's not fast enough to compete in respect of maximising profitability in relation to commuting downtime, and, more importantly, there aren't as many comforting buttons in it. The Rover 75 is a Vectra rival, but it's somehow not very businesslike. It's far too woody and pre-industrial for a bloke hell-bent on topping up the toner in your photocopier.

I set out to buy another car last week, having accepted, at last, that the old Bentley is just not suitable as everyday transport. Being a fan of comfort over performance, I started looking at secondhand execs. In fact, I had pretty much decided on a mid-90s BMW 7-series. They are terrific cars and an absolute steal, with a tidy high-miler costing as little as £6,000.

But when I drove one, I felt distinctly uneasy. In fact, I began to feel as though I was involved in something solutions-driven and committed to excellence. It completely spoiled the experience of an otherwise great car.

And do you know who I blame? David Brent and *The Office*. Someone recently gave me the whole first series on video, and just like everyone else I cringe behind the sofa every time he says vis-a-vis. Trouble is, I actually know people who talk a bit like that, and they all drive executive cars. Executive cars are driven by people like David Brent. Ricky Gervais has wiped thousands of pounds off the second-hand values of a whole sector of the car market

I can't drive a BMW 7-series. People might think I was on my way to a meeting. So I've bought an old Range Rover instead.

THE DUSTBIN OF AUTOMOTIVE HISTORY, OR THE 70s

Something very odd is going on where I live. Someone nearby has taken to driving around in a pristine Austin Allegro with a vinyl roof. Someone else down the road has recently acquired an Austin Princess. A bloke in the pub has been holding court about the pleasures of his early XJ S. And then, the other day, my woman told me that she wanted an original Vauxhall Cavalier. And it had to be gold.

I suppose this was bound to happen eventually. We've had the TV re-runs, seen the re-emergence of the flared trouser, and bought Led Zeppelin digitally remastered in a CD boxed set. It was only a matter of time before the spirit of Bodie and Doyle came crashing back into our lives in the shape of the 70s British car.

All of a sudden, 70s British cars are deeply fashionable, and apparently it's all to do with 'irony'. I admit that I was briefly drawn into all this, and only the other day found myself looking in the small ads at a 1974 metallic bronze Granada Ghia coupé for £1,500, and thinking how ironic it would be to drive around in it.

Then I thought a bit harder. I don't really know what irony is. I certainly couldn't explain it if I had to in a game of Articulate. But I'm fairly confident about what irony isn't. It isn't a Granada Ghia coupé. A Granada Ghia coupé is horrible.

In case the world is going mad and prices for original Talbot Tagoras are about to go through the roof, I want to make something absolutely clear. You shouldn't buy a 70s British car because it's ironic. You shouldn't buy a 70s British car because it's cool. And you shouldn't buy a 70s British car because you believe that it will offer a 'certain something' that a modern car doesn't. You should only buy a 70s British car if you're completely and utterly skint.

For a start, all old cars are essentially rubbish, otherwise they would still be in production. The viable motor car is a concept only just a hundred years old, so on the evolutionary scale a thirty-year-old car occupies the same position as a medieval cludgey does in the history of domestic plumbing. People who live in converted thirteenth-century abbeys fit modern lavatories. They don't make do with a cesspit out of a sense of irony and there's no excuse for having the automotive equivalent on your drive unless you are absolutely on your uppers.

Secondly, 70s British cars are especially bad because with one or two exceptions they were the work of men who wore donkey jackets and spent more time standing round a brazier than they did ensuring that your car was fit for purpose. The Rover SD1 may have been an inspired piece of design, but you can celebrate that with a poster. If you buy the real thing you will discover that, like a Lada, it was thrown together by a bunch of cack-handed communists.

Let's pause for a moment to consider the legacy of 70s Britain. The Ronco Buttoneer, the Sodastream machine, cheesecloth shirts, space hoppers and choppers, TV tennis games that went 'pip' and 'pop', the Advanced Passenger Train, Noddy Holder, Tupperware parties and *Are You Being Served?* We have not felt obliged to preserve any of these things, and I see no reason why we should suddenly make an exception for the Morris Ital. It was advertised on TV as being 'Styled in Italy and engineered in Britain', and the only way it could have been any worse was if they'd got that the other way around.

But wherever your 70s car came from it's going to break, because automotive technology and production methods only really came good in about 1990. I have recently driven a selection of 70s supercars for *Top Gear* TV and they all broke. The Aston Martin V8 Vantage lost a couple of blades from its radiator fan, so one moment I was driving the definitive 70s muscle car, but the next I was at the head of an enormous and embarrassing steamy road-comet.

Things weren't much better in Italy. The cockpit of the Lamborghini Countach filled with raw petrol vapour that interfered with my mind, so in some of the in-car commentary I sound a bit like Bob Dylan. The BMW M1 sheds bits of componentry at speed and the Ferrari 512BB wouldn't start at all. And these were bespoke cars endlessly pampered by wealthy enthusiasts. Imagine what a mainstream model with a moonshot mileage is going to be like.

If you're hard up, I sympathise. I'm a bit Bernie Flint myself at the moment, so I wouldn't discourage anyone from buying an old car if that's all they can stretch to. And if that means a Maxi, so be it. It will still be better than the bus. But please don't kid yourself that the Maxi is in any way clever, off-beat, alternative or, for Pete's sake, *ironic*. You're poor, and so your car is crap.

I know, because I drive a 70s Bentley T2. I drive a 70s Bentley because I can't afford a new one.

MOTOR INDUSTRY SUFFERS FROM INFERIOR INTERIOR COMPLEX

I'd like to spend this week talking about fabrics and interior design. It's therefore only fair to warn you that I'm not an authority on either of these things.

My house doesn't have any interior design. A single man's life really is far too short to admit any concerns over colour combinations or any of that Wang Chung stuff about harmony and balance. It's probably enough to point out that even though I've lived here for nearly four years, I've yet to remove the box of Tampax I found in the bathroom cupboard on the day I moved in (though largely for fear of invoking The Curse of the Previous Occupant). I really haven't got a clue about the world of interiors.

Mind you, I can't compose music in the style of JS Bach, but I know Bach when I hear it; and even though I can't cook succulent corn-fed breast meat with oyster mushrooms served under crisp pastry in an individual earthenware dish, I know a good chicken 'n' mushroom pie when I eat one. So I'm fairly confident in saying that the interiors of most new cars are bloody awful.

Let's be honest with ourselves here. It's all too easy to climb into a new car and think *ooh, what a nice interior.* Well, next time you do it, ask yourself this: would I buy a sideboard made out of beige plastic textured like a rhinoceros's buttocks? Would I have my sofa trimmed in a splinter-pattern multi-coloured fabric that brings on dementia? You would? Then buy the Citroen I was driving last week.

I know there have been one or two admirable efforts in recent years to improve the in-car environment. The Range Rover is perhaps the best blend yet of tradition and the sort of contemporaneity we expect of trendy hotel receptions. At the other extreme, Nissan has done some interesting work with fabrics, in the Micra, and Fiat with the feel of plastics, in the Idea. Bentleys still look pretty good in wood and leather because they've stuck with them from the start and seem to know what they're doing.

Elsewhere, though, things are a bit grim. If DFS produced furniture to the general standard of car interiors Michael Aspell would, finally, be out of a job.

For a start there are far too many cabins that appear to have been hewn from a single piece of coal. I drove the new Ford C-Max a while back. The ergonomics and lay-out of the inside were obviously very good, but I got the distinct impression that everything bar the hazard warning light switch was black. Practical and versatile it may be, but the atmosphere on board was like that depicted in Bruegel's *Death of the Virgin*.

At first I thought this might be a problem with national identity. Maybe a Japanese car should be more Japanese. Where is the tatami mat and the lacquer? Why do we not sit on the floor? Saabs and Volvos are rather dour and logical on the inside, which is an obviously Swedish attribute. But where is the slightly soggy wood from the sauna, and where the exposed fixings to give that unassailably Swedish air of self-assembly with an Allen key (not included)?

But then I realised this was twaddle. Whenever someone tries to build a truly British car they fill it with fake wood and floppy leather, and it looks silly. It's like trimming a Renault in Breton stripes and an onion motif to make it more French.

Here's another thought. In the past, your car's interior generally said something about the material sciences and fashions of the time. The cabins – or, rather, perches – of the first cars were made of wood, because that's what chairs were made of. Switches were made of brass, because switches just were. Bakelite was used for a time but by the

50s the new plastics were making an appearance – in the Citroen DS dashboard, for example.

I reckon the 60s was the decade of interesting trim advances. Cheap Fords had vinyl seats, because poor people had vinyl sofas. More expensive Fords may have had velour, because so did the G Plan recliner with its attendant pouffe. By 1969 the Rover P6 could be had with Formica door cappings, because Formica was the future.

But since then, nothing much seems to have happened. It's left to a few pieces of aluminium tinsel to make a cabin look something like the gadgets page from a men's magazine. Surely someone could do better than that?

Inexpensive furniture has come on in huge leaps in the last decade, but the average car interior seems to have gone nowhere. This is galling, since I'm obviously far more interested in the inside of my car than I am in the inside of my house. I want the interior of a car, any car, to be more like a dream home. I certainly want it to be a welcome relief from this one.

ALL THE NUTS ARE BROWN, AND THE TYRES ARE SHOT

On the 19 June 1978, an Italian-born but British-resident restaurateur by the name of Franco walked into a London motorcycle dealership and bought the Moto Guzzi he'd always promised himself.

It was an 850 T3 California: not an especially rare Guzzi and the event was not especially momentous in itself, even if the on-road price of £1,868.60 represented a lot of parmesan cheese back then.

Franco rode the Cali around for the next five years, falling off it once and bending the crash bars, until he had clocked up a leisurely 4,600 miles. And then, for reasons that are not entirely clear, he parked it in the back of his shed and completely forgot about it. Completely. He didn't cover it up, he didn't drain the fluids, he didn't even remove the ignition key. He just shut the door on a boyhood ambition he'd worked out of his system and went back to expanding his restaurant business.

The bike re-emerged over two decades later, when your humble correspondent and his mate Colin yoked it to the towbar of a van and dragged it, with a screech of protest from its seized brake pads, back into the light of a much-changed world. And, God in heaven, it looked bad.

It was very dusty. Quite a lot of it was rusty. The aluminium parts were more furry than a guardsman's headgear and the tyres had long since turned to coal. Here was probably the lowest-mileage California this side of Moto Guzzi's own museum and it looked like a motorcycle courier's spare bike.

But, as Henry Royce allegedly said to the Hon Charles Rolls when the latter asked why the car wouldn't start, 'she's already running'. The tyres have been replaced, the brake callipers and carburettors have been patiently stripped and rebuilt, there's a new battery under the seat and this morning, the California's odometer clicked past a heady 5,000 miles. It's one of three motorcycles I own and at the moment, it's my favourite.

But it still looks awful. Even cleaned up, it looks as though it came from the bottom of a canal. I'm not talking about an evocative patina of age, I'm talking about the sort of decay and ruin alluded to in the Old Testament.

What is to be done? On this point, Colin and I are divided to an extent that threatens our ancient friendship. He advocates dismantling the bike entirely and restoring it to better than new condition. My solution is to do absolutely nothing.

I know the classic bike fraternity will shudder at this, but let's think about it. Restoring the California would cost a lot more than simply buying a well-preserved original. It would probably take me five years. Something would snap or sheer off, and some important bits would be left over at the end of the comedy. I would end up with a nicer bike, but the story of its use, abandonment, decay and ultimate reprieve at my hands is recorded in the fabric of the thing, and all that would be lost to history.

Somehow, restoring the California would be a bit like scraping the patchy and faded fresco from the wall of an Italian renaissance chapel and replacing it with a laser-printed reconstruction. You'd get a more complete picture, but it wouldn't actually tell you as much as it did when it was falling apart.

The same mistake has been made with many old cars. At this year's Goodwood festival, I saw a few beautifully rebuilt 30s Mercedes racing cars. But in the Prague Technical Museum, they have one that was left there after the war and has never been touched. It is dented and scuffed, but ancient baked-on oil gives it a genuine reek of old glory and spent nationalist fervour. I hope they are never moved to so much as buff it up.

In fact, I think restoration may be terribly over-rated. We rebuild old houses and populate them with wax figures in period dress, but in doing so banish any lingering ghosts of the original inhabitants that may be present in the dust of the place. Natural history programmes show computer-generated images of how dinosaurs might have walked. It's all very clever, but I still find fossilised brontosaurus bones more exciting.

I find Franco's old bike strangely exciting, too. The more I look at it, the more I discover about the negligence of its previous owner, about the conditions under which it was stored, and even about the people who built it, since the way they put it together has had a bearing on the exact way it's falling apart. A restored California would be just another nice old bike, but a knackered one with only 5,000 miles on the clock has a story to tell.

People who visit castles will know what I mean. Windsor is magnificent, but the ruins at Corfe are more magical.

THE BROWN MOVEMENT, AND WHY IT SHOULD BE STAMPED ON

Brand values are obviously a complete con. If I've understood the history of motoring correctly, VW was founded on the principal of *ein car* for *ein volk*. And yet here they are, in 2003, producing a £65,000 limousine that nobody seems to want.

I've just spent a week with the W12 Volkswagen Phaeton and in many ways it knocked my face off. It presents a compelling case for being the most thoroughly engineered car in the world. Most objections to it, in fact, have centred around nothing more than the VW badge on the nose.

Being a VW doesn't make the Phaeton any less good; it may even make it better. But in any case, I've never been that bothered by a car's badge. I'm far more concerned about the colour.

And the first time I parked the Phaeton outside my house, and then glanced back at it as I walked away, something bothered me.

That evening, on my way to the pub, I had another look at it under the sodium streetlights. It still bothered me. Even when I re-emerged several hours later with my beer goggles on, I still didn't quite fancy it.

So the next morning I got up early and had a good hard stare at it in that watery first light that plays all sorts of tricks with the colour and shape of things. And I became very uneasy indeed. There was no longer any doubt in my mind. It was brown.

Now I've been around long enough to know that taste is a cyclic business. I've had my Adidas rucksack since I was at school, and after several decades in the loft it's resurrected as the envy of local youth.

I recently had a new kitchen fitted in my house, and I couldn't help noticing that my worktops are almost exactly the same colour as the ones my late grandmother had installed in her kitchen in the 50s. The light fittings, too, have an ancestral air about them.

Some years back I bought a job lot of six 60s refectory chairs in stainless steel and orange vinyl, for £20. I've now put them in the new kitchen and my wet friends walk in, gasp, and say 'Oooh, where can I get some chairs like that? They're so *now*.'

Actually, they're very then, but this is my point. The same thing is happening in car design. When I was a boy, chrome was cool. Then it wasn't, and people wanted matt black bumpers and plastic wheel trims to replace their shiny hub caps. Now the Vauxhall Vectra has a strip of chrome across its rump serving no purpose other than to celebrate the chrome renaissance.

We are simply witnessing one complete phase of the cycle, the phenomenon that causes old people at flea markets to pick up some overpriced item of old tat and exclaim 'Eeh, I must have had hundreds of these when I was young and I threw 'em all away.'

But I still believe that brown, at least as far as cars are concerned, was a one-hit wonder that did not become lodged on the great Wheel of Fashion. I know that red is the new black, fat is the new thin, short is the new long and mix is the new match, but I've yet to be convinced that brown is anything other than the same old brown. But I could be wrong.

So I rang Stephen Bayley, a chap who knows all about the vagaries of style and design, who has forthright views about things like Formica and who probably pronounces Anglepoise as if it were a French word.

And amidst a lot of stuff about Goethe and colour theory, he made a very interesting point. 'Brown is a very impure colour,' he said. 'It's not in the spectrum, so we're a bit suspicious of it.' How right he is.

I would go even further than that. Ignoring the obvious scatological connotations, brown is not the colour of motion, and as cars are essentially mobile things it just doesn't suit. Looking from the window of my office I can see no end of resolutely stationary brown things – the earth itself, for a start; house bricks, tree trunks, and my neighbour's dog. Brown has an innate static quality that made it perfect for the Fiat Strada but is wholly inappropriate on the 200 mph Phaeton.

Brown is fine on old overcoats, well-polished brogues, antique furniture and conkers, but these are organic products and their browns are many and varied, and forever changing with the play of light. The brown of a car body is not the same thing at all. It's unrelenting and so . . . well, it's just so bloody *brown*.

Car manufacturers, I'm told, are ready to give brown a second shot. They will not call it brown, of course, any more than they can bring themselves to call red anything other than 'richlieu'. It will be Sienna, Burnt Umber or Midnight Beige. But no one will be fooled.

Time and fickle fashion will change our view of most things motoring. Everything is relative and has to be viewed in the context of its era. Except brown. Brown, like the speed of light, is an absolute. It's absolutely awful.

SEEKING SOMETHING KNACKERED AND SHABBY – THAT'S MY GIRL

Ever since the E-type was given a preposterously long bonnet, men have secretly believed that driving a flash car will make them more attractive to women. You don't really need to be Germaine Greer to work this one out.

I've never liked to believe it myself, but then I would say that. Many years ago a girlfriend of mine admitted that she only went out with me because I had an Alfa Romeo, and that as I no longer had an Alfa Romeo, she'd be off now. At least it wasn't a purely physical thing.

Meanwhile, a discussion has broken out in the *Top Gear* office about what sort of car makes a woman more attractive to a man. My mate Hammond contends that a good car really does make a difference, citing, as an example, the Audi A4 Cabrio. This, he reckons, will do for any woman what Pilates, Botox or Atkins never can. He is actually on the record as saying the A4 Cabrio 'works a bit like beer'.

But I'm not so sure about all this. There is a trend for celebrity women these days to drive ludicrously flash motors – Jordan has a Bentley Azure, for example, and Jodie Kidd has a Lamborghini. And good for them, but isn't this all just a bit too predictable? And, more importantly, expensive?

No, what really does it for me is a slightly dishevelled arty bird with her own breasts driving something like a knackered Triumph Herald convertible. A nice girl in a crap car – it's the motoring equivalent of erotic naked mud-wrestling.

Right. I'm glad that's all sorted, because it means I can move on to the meat of this week's subject; buying a car for my girlfriend. She's one of these slightly dishevelled arty types, so I've allocated a very small budget to the exercise but only because, you understand, I don't want her driving around looking like a media tart.

Fortunately, her views on 'modern' cars are very encouraging. On being offered a drive in the Nissan 350Z: 'Ooh, how exciting. I've never been in a really dreadful car before.' At one point I considered buying a nearly new Alfa 156, thinking it was suitably alternative compared with the usual BMW/Audi fodder and a real enthusiast's car. I showed her one. 'If you're going to drive that, you may as well get a junior marketing job with Proctor and Gamble.' She looked so far down her nose at it I thought her head would snap clean off.

No, she likes old tat too, which is just as well under the circumstances. When she said she wanted 'an old Merc with saggy suspension' I almost kissed her. That would be easy.

In fact, I'd found one by the very next day – a 1969 250E. It was very solid, complete, fully functioning and in a decent period colour scheme. It was slightly faded but that was to be commended, as it kept the price down. It was looking quite promising until I discovered that the boot was full of water. 'Oh dear,' said the vendor. 'That seal must be leaking.' I said we'd go away and think about it.

Back in my own car, woman looked crestfallen. 'It's such a pity about the boot,' she said.

'Oh, not really. It probably just needs a new piece of rubber.'

But it was no good. By the time we'd rejoined the main carriageway the man had murdered his wife and buried her under the patio. And that meant everyone driving an old Mercedes was the same.

And, without wishing to bore you, that's how it goes on – each type of car is universally dismissed for some foible or failing on the part of the vendor we happen to encounter. Old Saabs are driven by earnest liberals. Old Volvos are driven by perverts. Old BMWs are driven by crooks, old

Fords by halfwits, and old VWs by people with BO. And that means if you buy one, you'll have BO as well.

All the money spent by these manufacturers on marketing and brand awareness has come to nought. A marque's image is dictated by the personal habits of the bloke selling an old one in the back of your local paper. Audi, for example, would have you believe they're a premium brand for people with taste. But fifteen years later you'll discover the harsh truth, which is that they're driven by people whose eyes are too close together to be trustworthy.

So Renault should take heart. Renaults are driven by decent people. And do you know how much a very usable early Renault 5 is these days? £200.

I know blokes who have spent more than that on supposedly sexy underwear. And I bet it didn't look half as good on.

FORTUNATELY, THE PAST ISN'T WHAT IT USED TO BE

He who will not learn from history is doomed to repeat it, said Socrates. Or was it Plato?

Tradition and the veneration of antiquity – these are reckoned to be British traits and I am glad of them. I love our heritage, but with qualifications. I am especially chuffed that there are people who sacrifice their spare time, income and marriages to the preservation of old motor cars, but I do not want to drive around in them. I recently stayed at Eastwell Manor, a beautiful Elizabethan house in Kent, but of course I did not want to live like an Elizabethan. I enjoyed lighting, running water, a fridge for my widget-equipped Boddingtons and freedom from pox and nonny-noing lutenists.

The great British marques go the way of the house. Look over and sit in a Jaguar and the company's heritage will assert itself like a grand old man who has retained his place on the board. But to drive and live with a Jaguar is a thoroughly modern experience. Moving abroad for a moment, the same is true of Alfa Romeo: the new Spider and GTV briefly doff their caps in deference to the Alfa tradition and then get on with being great new cars. Bravo. These makers survived and flourished because their pasts are a datum for progress, their traditional styling traits and driving characteristics merely a long tether on their designers' whims.

I would that our nation could go the way of these great car makers, for I am worried that the past is too much with us these days. Perhaps it's insecurity; perhaps it's a simple lack of courage; but Britain has become a nation rummaging through the archives, a people obsessed with the transient trappings of the past at the expense of the lesson of history.

It especially worries me that Rover has called its new roadster an MG. Here was a chance for one of our few surviving names to reassert itself in the nick of time with a fresh and independent product; instead it adorned it with a badge that disappeared years ago along with the irrelevant rubbish it had come to represent. Rover has felt obliged to do this because the British, and especially some sections of our motoring press, have been clamouring for a new MG when what we really wanted was simply a great new sports car – something altogether different. But then, in Britain we do not seem to want to build on the bedrock of the past, we want to replay it like an old film.

The television channels are clogged with retro serials and old sitcoms; the jukebox at my pub is stuffed with crappy 60s compilations with barely a new tune in earshot; our great towns are stagnating as tourist traps, littered with gifte shoppes to confirm that our retreat into nostalgia is ye right loade of olde nonfenfe.

Last week I bought a tin of ginger beer. It was decorated with a picture of frolicking, basin-haircut schoolboys in improbably long shorts reminiscent of snapshots of my grandpa's childhood. A tender reminder of the golden past we yearn for, perhaps? No – the artist had neglected to show the head lice, the rickets and the decline of the empire. Ominously, the drink that Enid Blyton stamped indelibly on our culture served only to make me flatulent.

I watched Morecambe and Wise – a mistake. Yes, they were brilliant, and yes, the Butler of the Year competition was one of the funniest things ever seen. But that was in the 70s. They are strangely not funny now, and my Rover P6 is no longer a good car.

Suddenly, our respect for antiquity has degenerated into wholesale foraging through the contents of a bin that no one has emptied for decades. And our motoring heritage, like your attic, is full of useless old junk.

BMW talks of reviving some of the other 'great' names of British motoring. Well, if Riley, Austin-Healey et al. were so great, where are they now? 'The government killed them,' cry some; 'They weren't managed properly,' insist others; 'The unions strangled them,' comes another disclaimer. But you know what? I've got a terrible feeling that they died because the cars, like the Monkees, cod liver oil and Spangles, were no longer good enough.

These names mean about as much now as Bile Beans – like MG, their philosophies and traditions burned out through neglect long ago. I am pleased that a few have been preserved: that way they can serve as a portent, warning our few extant makers against the perils of resting on one's laurels. But I urge BMW to be thoroughly German about this one and not pander to our ridiculous hankering for the past. BMW already has its own, living tradition of great car building and it may yet have saved Rover from the ignominious decline into badge engineering that claimed many of its coevals. So now, as Churchill once said on a poster, let us go forward together.

HE'S TERRIBLY BRITISH, YOU KNOW – EATS PIES

I wish to state straight off that I have nothing whatsoever against the Germans. Oh, very well, I think the Germans have been responsible for some of the worst haircut atrocities of the century and they eat far too many cakes, but I don't believe, as some do, that they are fundamentally evil people. It's just that they're not like us.

Right: the sale of our beloved Bentley. This is a subject on which I have, I believe, remained admirably silent, but now it's all over – and it is now – I am entitled to my two pfennigs' worth and here it comes.

What's more, I am driven to this by the actions of no less an institution than our own motoring press, which has continuously peddled the mealy-mouthed and treacherous assertion that selling our most revered brand to a bunch of Uhlans is essential for the future of the marque. But is it? There is an alarming tendency to treat this as a purely business issue when it may actually be something far more important – a cultural one. BMW is undoubtedly very good at making cars; in purely empirical terms it makes better cars than Bentley. But the point is that it makes very good BMWs. This leads us to the eternally vexing question of what makes a British car British.

Here we come up against another popular misconception – that it's all about wood, leather and radiator grilles. But that, I'm afraid, is a bit of spineless appeasement. You could trim the Continental R – one of my favourite cars – in formica and cheesecloth and it would still be terribly British. It is something far more complex than I or even the undoubtedly clever Germans could codify, but I'm going to have a go anyway.

British car design has something to do with a slight brutality of form and function, a certain lumpiness even. The Continental is a very elegant shape but it's magnificence has a crushing quality to it and not just because it's big and heavy. Even small British cars – Mini, Austin Healey Sprite – are thick-set, in both their aesthetics and their dynamics.

You are now positively quaking with the urge to point out that a lot of great British cars past were, in fact, penned by foreigners. I know. The DB Astons were shaped largely by Italians; even the six-cylinder engine was the work of a displaced Pole. Some of the most wonderful and exclusive Derby Bentleys were actually clothed in French bodywork. But Touring of Milan, to take the Aston example, were internationally minded people working to a brief and in any case, such people were stylists rather than design engineers, a distinction that reflects the different nature of car manufacture in an earlier age.

My guts tell me that the Britishness of the DB5 was cemented long before the bodywork was considered. It was somewhere in the mechanical philosophy, perhaps; weights, wheelbase, bores and strokes, I don't know – I said this was too difficult. But *something* of a fundamentally British nature was there influencing the work of the people who clothed these great cars – how else do you explain that a DB Aston is so different from a contemporary Ferrari, even though both are superficially the work of Italians?

Somehow, a great British car seems to have evolved from the ground up. A great Italian car is created with a few deft and committed strokes of an artist's brush, but a great British one is somehow wrought and has a dose of Nelson's blood and sweat in it.

To my mind, it is this unmistakable industrial quality that distinguishes Britishness, and it's not just true of cars. Take Triumph's current range of motorbikes – they, too, are very British, despite the widespread accusation that the new Triumph has merely reversed the copy engineering techniques that saw the name formerly vanquished by Japan.

Look at the highly acclaimed T595 sportbike – it's not beautiful, it's rugged, bold and handsome. Look at the size of the bloody fuel tank.

Come to think of it, look at the size and shape of our standard beer glass; look at the Doctor Marten boot; look at meat and potato pie and compare it with a bowl of airy fairy penne al pesto. You see, Britishness in car design cannot be viewed in isolation, it's just one branch of a complex national psyche with distant origins in history, breeding, probably even the weather. The Germans' is closer to ours than many countries' – they eat lots of sausages as well – but *it's not the same*. So just how long will British car design last when it's no longer rooted in the conscience of The People? We could end up with something neither truly British nor reassuringly German, and for the first time both teams could be the losers.

Those – and I fear this could include a good many Germans – who imagine the essence of Britishness can be preserved in a few affectations of trim are the same people who would turn this once great nation into a museum, festooned with brown road signs, bag-in-a-cup tea, sticky buns and a crappy visitors' centre on every corner.

I am due to drive the new Arnage any day now and I'm pretty sure I'm going to love it. It would appear to be, with the exception of a few odds and sods, a distinctly domestic product. It was, after all, conceived long before the issue of the company's ownership was raised. Bentleys will continue to be made in this country for a long time yet; but is that enough to ensure that a Bentley remains a British thing?

Let's look further ahead by looking back at the Rover 600. Here was an essentially foreign car festooned with a few expedient traditional trappings and proclaimed as the return of the old Rover we knew and loved. I drove it a lot at launch and actually thought it was a nice car. But I never for one moment thought it was genuinely *British*. It was a Japanese tourist in a bowler hat.

And my worry now is that Bentley will become just another German in suspect leather gear.

OURS ARE BAD, BUT IVAN'S IS TERRIBLE

Everybody, even people with no interest whatsoever in motoring matters, has an opinion on what is the best car in the world. You do, I do, and my woman, who generally differentiates between cars only on the basis of colour, is adamant that the greatest expression of automotive art is the so-called Orange Volkswagen Beetle. On this, we differ.

But no matter: it's a healthy enough debate and one set to rage in pubs for as long as there are cars on the road. Meanwhile, landlords will be pleased to know, I can free up a good deal of uninterrupted drinking time by offering a definitive candidate for worst car in the world, ever.

It is a car I alluded to a few weeks ago and described as 'pretty crappy' with some authority, being the only Western journalist I know to have driven one. Then, I was relying on a three-year-old memory of a trip to Nizhny Novgorod, Russia. I now write to you once more from the former USSR to confirm that the GAZ Volga saloon is, as they say in these parts, utterpantski.

The Mahindra Jeep may be a quantitatively worse piece of engineering, but that is just an expediency for the owners of Indian tea plantations. The Volga was, in the Soviet system of things, a posh car for middle-ranking party officials, Aeroflot executives and the like. The proles had a Lada or Moskovitch, if they were lucky, while toffs got a Chaika or even a Zil limo. The Volga, then, is a sort of Russian Rover 800, but there even that unpromising comparison ends. It really is Grimsky Korsakov.

Five minutes in a Volga is enough to remind you that it is the product of a country suffering the mutually aggravating problems of being both a very grim place and one in which it is terrifyingly easy to get absolutely plastered for about 25p.

Inside the Volga, the hard and hideously cheap dash mouldings gleam dully like the elbows of my geography teacher's sports jacket. Knobs and controls appear to be pilfered from a variety of old Soviet kitchen appliances and there is always at least one missing. The footwells are often finished in linoleum. Radio reception is generally bad behind the old iron curtain but it's worse in a Volga. The engine reputedly has six cylinders and uses petrol but always sounds like a diesel twin. The panel gaps are so woeful that cats can probably work their way into a parked Volga for a crafty kip.

On the move, the Volga's rear suspension is revealed to be located with a couple of split pins and in most versions is formed from leaf springs you'd hesitate to use on a hand cart. Traverse a series of sharp undulations and the body will still be bouncing around as you climb out at your hotel. Yo heave-ho on the steering wheel and discover the inspiration for *The Song of the Volga Boatmen*. In fairness, the Volga's most recent incarnations have been dragged into the early 60s with a semblance of independent rear suspension and a general rounding off of corners, but even so, observing the evolution of the Volga must have been like waiting for a new TV under Brezhnev. In a free-market economy that now offers its citizens the opportunity to buy a Daewoo Leganza, it's just bloody well not Boris Godunov.

That, then, concludes my assassination of the GAZ Volga saloon. Yet we are only three-quarters of the way through this column so there must be a big 'but' attached to all this, and there is.

But, for some reason, I love Volgas. They have the enduring charm that comes only with truly pathetic things – stray puppies, broken children's toys, Italian plumbing – and, above all, the Volga approach works. Volgas are, after all, extremely long lived for cars that essentially leave the production line as scrap – it's not unusual to see 50s models chugging around. They feature only a handful of moving parts and they're all made of pig iron, so while nothing on them ever works entirely properly, nothing ever seems to break completely, either.

European imports to the former Soviet countries are invariably modified with sturdier springs and raised ride heights to cope with roads that appear to have been subjected to heavy shellfire over the last few days. The Volga's rudimentary suspension, however, allows it to crash straight through as if bound for Berlin, adding to the damage as it goes.

Ignition modifications are also often required of foreign offerings; the Volga's engine is wonderfully under-stressed and designed to run on horrible Russian petrol from the start, so it will probably run on any vaguely volatile fluid right down to and including the driver's urine which, for reasons intimated earlier, is probably about 80 per cent proof anyway.

Crap, yes. The worst car in the world. Outstandingly pragmatic, though. Any chance that GAZ could put in a bid for Longbridge?

VOLVO DRIVERS FAIL TO SHAKE OFF HAT STIGMA

As a teenager, I desperately fancied this girl called Liz. After several weeks of perseverance, she agreed to come to the pictures with me but only on the understanding, it was made quite clear to me as I stood trembling outside the tradesman's entrance, that her father drove us to the cinema and came to collect us again afterwards. Imagine my horror, then, when he wheeled a Volvo 240 from the garage and proceeded to drive it in what can only be described as a hat.

We all know about old blokes who drive in hats. They are the sort of people who look through, rather than over, the steering wheel and in cars that appear to have run away unattended but for the presence of a trilby just above the door tops. People who drive in hats have firm views on driving techniques that are firmly rooted in 1960. Which, as it happens, is also the last time they looked in the rear-view mirror. Hatted drivers occupy motoring's moral high ground and no doubt a similar position in the rest of life too. A man who drove a Volvo 240 in a titfer was not going to allow me free rein with his daughter. In fact, he wouldn't even let me in the house after sundown.

Some cars attract hats in the way old Escorts attract dodgy alloys. Most famously there was the Austin Allegro, which I remain convinced came with a brown hat as standard equipment. Its mantle, and its headgear, appears to have been adopted these days by the Toyota Starlet. And I can't help noticing the odd Lexus LS400 flaunting that essential wide-brimmed accessory. When I was a lad a Volvo was never fully dressed without a hat, either. But that was a long time ago.

These days, as we all know, Volvos are cool. Even people my age have Volvos and I don't know anyone who routinely sports a homburg. As it happens, a Volvo C70 convertible has today been delivered for my appraisal and, by a strange coincidence, I have also received a press release from its manufacturer concerning the very same car. Most curiously of all, this missive is advising me to wear a hat.

I couldn't believe it. 'Volvo', it says, 'is advising drivers of its new C70 convertible to wear hats.' Admittedly, it goes on to say '. . . to protect their delicate scalps from the sun's harmful rays' but I still thought it was a bit much. The note comes with a series of pictures of some olive-skinned stunner modelling a selection of recommended fashion items and she looks terrific. But do not be fooled.

I have in my wardrobe a selection of hats acquired all around the world. For the purposes of researching this column I have tried them all on in front of the mirror and, without exception, they make me look a total tool. The American baseball cap immediately halves my IQ; the Australian one makes me look like a bloke in search of a horse and the straw one makes me look like a luvvie between jobs. And so on. Hats do this to most people.

And yet here is Volvo, of all people, advising you to put one on in their new motor car – an open motor car at that – so that you may announce to the world that you are not the perceptive, style-literate individual that your choice of wheels suggests but, in fact, a berk.

This press release gets worse. Following the initial appeal to violate your own head it goes on to talk about skin cancer. This is the first press release I have received from a car maker that mentions disease. I realise that skin cancer is a growing concern in the West but I don't need Volvo telling me about it because that is the job of the British Medical Association whilst Volvo's task is to build ever more appealing cars and banish its ninnyish, over-protective reputation for good. Hats my arse (if you see what I mean): just because the sun has got one on doesn't mean the rest of us have to follow suit.

'We at Volvo are obviously concerned about the safety of our customers . . .' Yes, obviously. We know this following several generations of cars not yet passed away which were designed with a ruler and a pencil because the remainder of the development budget had been spent on impact-absorbing bumpers.

Open advocacy of hat-wearing in cars could knock Volvo's reputation right back to the era when I trundled off in abject misery to see *The Spy Who Loved Me*. I keep hearing that Volvo has changed its image and overall I believe it to be true. But the moral of the story is: if the hat fits, wear it.

HONDA – AT THE CORE OF THE HUMAN CONDITION

No one seems to know exactly which Little Honda the Beach Boys had in mind when they penned the rock 'n' roll classic of that name in 1964, but as it's of the same vintage, I wonder if it might be the C200 currently parked on my drive.

I bought this widow-maker a few weeks ago, from a mate who is into such things, on a whim, and for a few hundred pounds. If this is the one, then I have to say it's undermined my faith in the Beach Boys even more than the phrase 'two-wheel bike' did when first I heard it. Formed mainly from pressed tin, matt black and patinated with rust, the local young people clearly think the C200 is about as groovy as herpes.

Its shortcomings start with the nomenclature. The Honda CB1300 I was riding a few weeks ago has an engine of roughly 1,300 cc. The CB750 had a 750 engine. The 250 Superdream had a 250 cc engine. And yet the C200 turns out to have a 90 cc engine. Why? Power is quoted at 6.5 hp, but in practice is negligible, especially as a closer examination of the owner's manual reveals that this 90 cc engine in fact displaces just 87 cc. This is the sort of thing Japan should apologise for.

So it doesn't go especially well but, then again, it doesn't really stop either. Squeeze the tiny lever back to the bar and the cables leading to the front drum brake can be seen flexing and tensing like the sinews of a weightlifter. But nothing happens. This probably wasn't a problem in 1964, since back then no one else could stop either. But these days I might be behind the sort of fecund youth who stands his scooter on its nose for a laugh, or an idiotic Porsche Boxster owner who has specified the ceramic discs.

And why is it so ludicrously small? I realise that in the early 60s poor people still had rickets and ate coal, but it can't have made that much difference, surely? If I stretch across the tank in an effort to extract more speed from this 87 cc powerhouse, my chin is illuminated by the headlight. Motorcyclists are fond of saying how they 'wear' a really responsive bike; how the suspension and engine seem synaptically connected to them. Riding the Honda C200 is more like wearing a pair of undersized Y-fronts. To say that the CB1300 feels absurdly large after the C200 is to understate the magnitude of the problem. Cutlery feels big.

So – it doesn't really go, it barely stops and it makes me look ridiculous: all knees and elbows projecting, like the teacher from the Bash Street Kids on his bicycle. It smells of old metal, the neighbours hate it, and teenagers line the streets to deride my progress on it. On any logical level, it's simply something that someone forgot to scrap.

You will have noticed, though, that we're only about two-thirds of the way through this column, so you're expecting one of those big 'however' moments. However, on this occasion I've decided to go for an 'and yet' instead.

And yet . . . it's still a real motorcycle. It still does the job, in the way that, as much as I love a good bhuna, a tin of Spam would be enough if I were marooned and starving. The gulf between the C200 and the CB1300 may seem a huge one, but it is a hairline crack compared with the gulf between it and waiting for a bus. It represents a dependable and elemental freedom of a kind Soichiro Honda understood only too well, and the pop-pop of its feeble exhaust was once the distant rumble of an invasion force approaching from the East.

If automotive luxury could be defined as a reassuring excess of everything – power, space, chilled air, sound insulation, the depth of a seat cushion – then the Honda C200, in its ruthless expediency, perhaps represents the truth. It's the least you can get away with, which lends its clattering single piston and crimped-together pressed-steel frame a sort of nobility. Riding the C200 is in one way a deeply sobering brush with austerity, in another it feels like a victory for pragmatism over the demons of fashion, aspiration and excess.

Apologies for once again dragging out a croaked poet to help make my point but, long before the motorcycle was even invented, Thomas Gray expressed it all perfectly in his famous elegy:

> The boast of heraldry, the pomp of power,
> And all that beauty, all that wealth e'er gave,
> Awaits alike th' inevitable hour –
> The paths of glory lead but to the grave.

The little Honda will lead you there just as certainly.

THE ART OF DRIVING

WANTED: GRADUATE TRAINEE TO WORK AS PUNCHBAG

D angerous places, attics. Apart from the obvious risk of putting your foot through the ceiling, as dad once did with dire consequences for the Airfix models I'd hung from it, you never know what you might find. An advert for a loft conversion company runs something like: *searching for a paintbrush, I found a studio* – the reality is that you go up there innocently enough looking for an old book and end up having to confront some hideous reminder of your past which you'd hoped to banish. Come to think of it, that was exactly why I hid my school reports up there in the first place.

But even *James is unlikely to achieve maturity* did not fill me with quite the same loathing as another personal effect found in the same box. It was nothing more than a faded payslip, dated almost exactly ten years ago and denoting the princely take-home remuneration of £380 for the first month in my first job after leaving university. Yet with the crinkly print-out in my trembling hand I found myself crouched in the darkest corner of the attic of my mind, having unwittingly lifted the lid on a tight bundle of memories which I had intended to leave undisturbed for ever. It was, you see, a job in the motor trade.

I was employed as the Service Centre Administrator for a ... um, let's just say it was a franchised dealer for a well-known marque. I was of course the receptionist, but that title did not sit so well with the advertised status of graduate trainee even if the nylon blazer and consequent regular electrocution by the filing cabinet did. And as a receptionist I quickly learned the golden rule of all service industries, namely that the customer is often wrong. That I could deal with, but as the business was almost invariably wrong as well I ended up like a soldier stuck in no-man's land when both lines of trenches hide an enemy.

On the left flank, the angry customer; on the right, afforded protection by a wall and a door with a permanently oily handle, the bloody-minded technicians who never had to deal with one Mr Harvey and his absurd requirement actually to mend his car this time. Fortunately, I arrived too late to witness a (oops, nearly mentioned a name) large saloon car falling from the hydraulic ramps and landing on its roof just moments before the owner side-stepped reception and wandered into the workshop to see how things were going. What would I have said? We're just checking the underseal, sir. This would at least have been a suitable initiation, as might the sunroof that turned out to be considerably smaller than the hole cut for it. My turn came soon enough, though.

He was a valued customer, an elderly bloke who walked with a stout stick owing to some old leg wound. His headlight wipers didn't work, but they'd obviously simply worked loose on the splined shafts of their motors. Come back this afternoon and it will be fixed, sir. He came back, I flicked the switch to demonstrate a job done well, and the wipers gave one desultory swipe before dropping off altogether. Suddenly – miraculously, even – he was possessed of two good legs, thus freeing his walking stick for the job, once he'd cornered me on the forecourt, of beating me around the head.

I could continue for months with the largely unbroken series of sit-com catastrophes that characterised my six months at, ahh, Cockups of Cackford and of which the wiper incident was merely the first. As I type, my hands turn clammy as the sound of a severed door mirror, the sight of oily thumbprints on pale hide and the threatening phone calls reverberate down the years, but even set in context the radio incident stands out.

She was another regular and arrived in reception unexpectedly, clutching a new and expensive radio/cassette. Could we fit it? The workshop was fully booked (I always said that, it helped mentally prepare the customer for disappointment) but I'm sure we could. It was a simple enough job. Come back at the end of the day. Later, I was pleased to note the new unit fitted and the old one lying on the passenger seat.

She returned incensed. Why hadn't we done it? And where was the new radio? I examined the car to discover that, incredibly, someone had put the old one back in. The new one was nowhere to be found. I was genuinely baffled by this until, the next day, another client rang to say he was well pleased with the first service on his new car, especially the new radio. He hadn't realised there was anything wrong with the old one.

Looking back, maybe all this was the way of the real world and I really hadn't achieved sufficient maturity to deal with it. Then again, perhaps the place was just a bloody shambles in accordance with the reputation of so many franchised garages. I met a service receptionist the other day. He was sweating under a similar blazer whilst trying to explain to a friend why his car had sat unattended in the car park all day. My friend seemed unduly angered by the whole thing; personally, I wouldn't have let it worry me. They all do that, sir.

TURN ON, TUNE IN, BUGGER ME IF IT ISN'T *THE ARCHERS*

Anyone who believes that Britain is being dumbed down need only spend an hour listening to Radio 3 to be reassured that it isn't.

Forget Classic FM – it has soap-powder adverts on it and too many celebrity presenters playing too much Vivaldi. Vivaldi is for bookshops and vegetarian restaurants, not serious mental stimulation.

No, Radio 3 is hard work, which is exactly as it should be. The Radio 3 transmitter, wherever it is, is an immutable and unassailable beacon of unadulterated intellect. It is said that only cockroaches will survive the nuclear holocaust, but I'm not so sure. I bet there will be an ancient Roberts Radio as well, and a bloke oblivious to the catastrophe all around, still trying to explain exactly what Schoenberg was up to. I love Radio 3. It makes me feel small.

What a pity it's no good in the car. For a start, it has too many pauses; not just the ones between movements of Beethoven, but also the ones between Beethoven and presenter. You can tune into the third programme in the car and drive for several miles believing the radio to have packed up.

Another problem is that I can never turn off the traffic announcement function on a modern car radio. Bach did not score the Orchestral Suites for strings, soloists and news of a tailback delivered fortissimo and in the bombastic style of Radio Shropshire. It always spoils the artistry of the moment.

Finally, there is the issue of dynamics. Unless you are in something seriously quiet and refined – the Rolls-Royce Phantom perhaps – you're going to miss half of it anyway. You can crank up the slow movement of Mahler as high as you like, but you still won't hear it. And when the third movement starts the doors will fall off and your eardrums will cave in.

So – I can't listen to Radio 1 because I'm now too old to understand it. I can't listen to Radio 2 because it sounds like Radio 1 did when I was young, which makes me miserable. So that leaves Radio 4.

And a lot of Radio 4 is very good. Or at least, it is when I listen to it in the kitchen. However, I am absolutely convinced that a different Radio 4 is beamed to cars, and it's essentially *The Archers*. I never hear *The Archers* in the home, but within five minutes of driving off in the car we're going over to Ambridge with the cheesy theme tune. Da da-da, da-da, da-daaaah. It's the ruin of England.

God, I hate *The Archers*. It's an insidious blight of broadcasting that seeks out the cabin of a humble hatchback and a leather-lined supercar alike. There is no escape from the Grunties or the Grumbles or whatever those peasanty ones are called.

Come on, fans of Ambridge – I know there are millions of you out there. What's so good about it? Write in and tell me. It's rubbish, surely? It's hammy, hackneyed and completely cringeworthy. Even thinking about it makes me cross.

Nobody really talks like that. And what's with this unflagging quest to introduce contentious sociological issues to a programme about farmers? The war, the countryside and how people in the big city don't understand it, foreigners, gay people, drugs – sooner or later they all make an entry with a clunk like a big end failing.

One of my favourite in-car games is to see if I can drive through a whole episode of *The Archers* without losing my temper. I've never managed it. Instead, I've nearly written off a Bentley, an Aston Martin and a number of German executive saloons through radio rage.

I can't imagine anyone who actually lives in the cuds listening to *The Archers*. This would be a bit like me sitting in my house in West London and listening to a programme about town folk who worry over putting the bins out on time and finding a parking space. *The Archers*, judging by the listeners I know, is for twee and misty-eyed middle-class urbanites who cling to some fluffy misconception of the English rural idyll.

Well, let me tell you something. It's not even accurate. I've just spent a weekend in the countryside, and although much of it looks very pretty at a distance, it's actually pretty horrible close up. It's wet and very muddy and smells of cows. It's too dark, there are no shops, and it isn't even peaceful. There's always a dog barking or something being shot somewhere.

I now firmly believe that we should build more nice roads in the countryside. How else can we admire it in safety if not from our cars? The countryside is for driving through. In silence. I don't want to live there, not even vicariously.

I CAN DRIVE A FERRARI BECAUSE I'M LIGHT ON MY FEET

I often think that life would be a lot easier if I could just be an Italian. For example, as an Englishman, my tax return is an annual trauma because I've been meticulous and honest with my finances and I believe in playing it straight. But if I were Italian I could dismiss the whole thing with an emphatic shrug, because all the money would be in used notes under the bed.

You think I'm making this up? Just before Italy switched to the new Euro there was a huge surge in domestic car sales, and all because the people needed a way to dispose of all their undeclared lira.

My brief experiences of Italian industry are very encouraging, too. The working day begins with a cappuccino, followed by some crostini, then an argument and an espresso and then it's lunchtime. Lunch is enormous, lasts for two hours, probably involves some grappa and is followed by a kip, by which time we can start thinking about going home. Somewhere in the middle of all this is a one-hour work break when you might be engaged in building an Alfa Romeo, or some similar casual job.

The best argument for converting to Italy, however, is this: if I were an Italian, I would be able to drive a Ferrari in my normal shoes.

The last Ferrari I drove was a BB512, and experience warned me that even my lightest, snuggest-fitting and least substantial English bench-made brogues would be far too big for the Fezza's pedal box. And I was right: the box the shoes came in would have been bigger.

I can drive my old Bentley in my coarsest builder's gang-boots, which is exactly how most of them are driven, come to think of it. The Bentley's pedals are like the treadles of a Victorian workhouse. A Ferrari's are just too small for anyone with proper peasant breeding.

As something of a footwear fetishist, this bothers me. I have spent quite a bit of time roaming those exquisite little shoe shops you find in the back streets of Milan and Turin, some of which have even been open. The Italians make some fantastic shoes, but I have never bought any. That's because I'm a size eleven, and all Italian men are size seven. I'm surprised they can even stand up.

Japanese men are all size five, though in fairness to them they do fall over quite a bit, especially on a Friday night in the bars and jazz clubs of Roppongi. Yet even they have recognised that properly bred northern Europeans with a hint of Viking in them have proper feet, so they build their cars accordingly. I can drive the Honda NSX in any of my shoes.

Back with the 512, I had two choices. I could have bought a pair of those high-performance Puma racing bootees, as favoured by the supercar fraternity. Trouble is, they tend to be rather gaily coloured and give the impression that you're walking around with a couple of miniature sports motorcycle fairings strapped to your feet. They also cost in excess of £120, and for that sort of money I could buy a nice pair of shoes. I wasn't going to spend £120 just to look like the sort of man who knows how to heel and toe.

So in the end, as usual, I was forced to rummage in the cupboard under the stairs and dig out my ballet shoes.

Now I wish to point out straight away that I have never been a ballet dancer. But I did once, and for a reason that now escapes me, find myself at a Royal Opera House jumble sale of redundant ballet costumery. I could have bought Romeo's billowing shirt or Julliet's tutu, but instead I headed straight for the footwear section.

Most dancers, like Italians, have woefully small feet. An exception is William Tuckett, a former Royal Ballet soloist and a man who, by the standards of his profession, has gallumping great plates of meat. I tried a pair of his old bootees. They fitted perfectly. In fact, they fitted better than my socks.

I was immediately struck by some similarities between the dance boot and the racing boot. Tuckett's were superbly made out of the most supple leather I have ever had the privilege to slip over an unworthy foot and had clearly never been worn outdoors. The soles were stiff but thin, for heightened feedback.

There were also some differences. I had to acknowledge that the ballet boots were finished in a sort of pixie green and had tassels on them, but as these weren't long enough to interfere with braking, it wasn't really an issue. They weren't fireproof either, but as I wasn't planning to set light to them this didn't bother me one bit. So I queued up with a load of old women clutching Darcy Bussell's used underwear and bought them.

Of course, whenever I climb manfully out of the cabin of a gently smoking Italian supercar I give the impression that I've just come from an am-dram performance of *Snow White*, but I don't care. It's a small price to pay for being able to brake for a roundabout without accelerating straight into the chevrons.

And my detractors – there are many – might like to consider this. Turn a boot over and, on the sole, you can read the inscription 'Tuckett, Duke, Beauty' – they were worn by Mr Tuckett in the role of the Duke in the early 90s production of *Sleeping Beauty*. This may seem irrelevant, but if there was a Goodwood Festival of Ballet they would be described as unique boots with a documented dance pedigree. In second-hand ballet-wear terms, this is the equivalent of owning a Birdcage Maserati that was once driven by Fangio in the Mille Miglia.

If this was a pair of race boots formerly worn by Schumacher in a Formula One race, they would probably be sold by Bonhams and Brooks for several thousand pounds at a posh auction in Monaco. But the price of the Duke's boots, the best driving boots ever made? Ten pounds.

Remarkable, really, because if you look beyond the price difference and the thorny issue of colour scheme, there really is very little to distinguish the two types of boot. One is a bespoke item hand-crafted from the finest materials in the interests of supremely deft footwork, and lent extra kudos through having once been used in anger by an absolute master of his art. The other is just a pair of poncy overpriced trainers.

ALL YOU NEED TO KNOW WHEN DRIVING IN FRANCE

I don't know if anyone out there has driven through France lately, but if you haven't, I'd keep it that way.

I accept that this will be an unpopular suggestion. I realise that the British middle classes like nothing more than affecting a deep Francophilia and hiring a nice little villa in a 'wonderful' cheese region for the summer, and pronouncing Côte du Rhône in a way that suggests they have a big docker's oyster to get rid of.

And yes, I know: you can find a lovely little cafe at the roadside serving a really nice cassoulet and it's so cheap I couldn't believe it and those motorway tolls really work you know we went all the way from Paris to the Loire Valley and never saw a traffic jam once it's because their public transport is so good our government should go to France and see how it's done I love France I think I'd like to buy a little house there one day the property prices are so reasonable compared with here and the way of life I mean it's so relaxed and the bread – ooooh!

But that's not the point. You'll be killed.

I've just driven all the way back from the South of France to the Main Land in the new BMW 645Ci, and I am now more convinced than ever that we will never achieve true European unity. Like all great undertakings that come to nought, the project will founder on something very simple and close to the hearts of the people, and in this case it's the total, utter and complete inability of the French to drive cars.

I've been observing the phenomenon of French driving for many years now, but being reasonable, tolerant, liberal minded and loth to generalise, and having in any case won the lottery of life, I've kept my mounting concerns to myself. But now I've had enough, and I'm ready to speak forth on this subject. So read carefully, for I shall write this only once.

They're crap.

Statistics suggest that the Italians are crap as well, but there is a difference. The Italians manage to drive badly with a certain amount of panache. A senior executive of the Italian motor industry once told me that a red light in Naples is an 'advisory signal'. Naples is the sort of place where you stop at a green light in case someone is coming the other way.

The Germans? They can be very aggressive but because they're German they manage to drive aggressively with a degree of precision. The Spanish are pretty bad drivers as well, but as they're all too busy sleeping or sitting on a chair on the pavement for no apparent reason, it's rarely an issue.

The French are just rubbish. A recent newspaper report suggested that one in ten French drivers may not have a licence. I'd be amazed if the figure was that low. France is a much larger country than ours and has fewer cars in it, so it's a bit of a mystery why the one behind has to be so close. In Britain we invented something called the two-second rule, but the French seem to have mistakenly converted this to metric and arrived at 5.08 centimetres.

You cannot drive anywhere in France without a French driver right up your arse. Whether you're out on a country road or overtaking a line of slow lorries on a dual carriageway, he'll be there, a-weaving and a-flashing as if he's got something more important to get to than a coffee and a calvados.

Because the French are all socialists and generally given to a scaffold-building mentality, they reserve their worst driving for such time as they come across a nice, shiny, new and undamaged motor, particularly if it's being driven by a foreigner and especially an Englishman. You will cruise gently past a French driver in an old Renault on the Autoroute, then the instant you arrive at a winding mountain road he will try to overtake you on that blind off-camber corner where you pulled out to make room for an old peasant on a bicycle.

And they're always banging on about how it's more correct to drive on the right. Really? At anything even vaguely approximating to a left-hander, they drive straight down the bloody middle anyway. Useless.

I mean, have you seen the state of the cars in France? I have never seen one without a big dent in it, even obviously new ones. I'm absolutely convinced that they must go over them with a hammer while they're still in the showroom, just to get it over with. French visitors to Britain must be amazed at how smooth and evenly rounded a typical Peugeot is. They've never seen one like that before.

My mate Hamster contends that the core of a typical French car is reasonably solid but that all the extraneous fittings – bumpers, wheel trims and what have you – will fall off. This makes sense, since all those bits are regarded as consumables by the French and are only really put there for the export market. Indicators are for the export market as well.

Let's take parallel parking. You or I would find a space a few feet longer than the car and then reverse into it with due care and attention. The French, meanwhile, drive around all day in search of that elusive spot that's slightly shorter than the car. They lunge in nose first and shunt to and fro until all the lights are broken and one wheel is on the pavement, then step out and shrug their shoulders as if the whole thing was beyond their control. Which it was, in fact.

Let's face it – they just can't do it. I dare say they do some nice *croque monsieur* on the motorway but until they can sort out the driving, I shall continue to regard France as somewhere I have to drive through in order to get to Italy,

And from now on, I'm not driving through it in my own car. Instead of buying a nice little property on the south coast, I'm going to buy a horrible little Renault 5 and leave it in France for such time as I have to go there.

You might wonder where I'm going to keep it, but don't worry. I've been to France often enough to know that I can just park it on a roundabout somewhere.

SHEEP – A WASTE OF GOOD WOOL

This month, I have acquired a cat. He's a black and white tom, eight weeks old, and I have named him Fusker in memory of the late Bob Cook, father of my childhood friend Robert Cook. He was a man who hated cats.

In fact he would refer to any cat as 'a little fusker' and it's only now I realise that he was probably just sparing Mrs Cook's blushes. But it's too late. He answers to Fusker, I love him, and he loves me.

But don't worry. I'm not going to turn into one of those pathetic pussy-whipped blokes who says 'Ha ha it was ever so funny the other day with Fusker he climbed onto my desk and jumped onto the computer keybolrddgdfgk lsdkfj l sdf k sdfsldfkjjjjjjj and I said look Fusker there's a mouse and he chased it ha ha ha and I lost everything!'

In any case, I seem to have come by the world's least intelligent moggie. Traditionally they like radiators and patches of warmth on the tiled floor where the sunlight slants through a window, but the other day – it was ever so funny – I opened the fridge to get another beer and found I'd shut him in it! And he was purring!

In the end, even the most ardent cat fancier would have to admit that they just aren't very bright. They have become the stuff of superstition, various cultures have attributed mystical powers to them, and the ancient Egyptians went as far as to turn a cat into a deity. My own exerience, however, suggests that the cat understands only two things – the peerless pleasure of a fresh dollop of Whiskas, and the pain of being trodden on following a mistimed lunge at an approaching booted foot.

Mind you, compared with some sheep I've met recently Fusker is Magnus ruddy Magnusson.

I've been meeting a lot of sheep, because I've been driving in Scotland and Wales. I liked them. They're decorative and scenic; they wander, lonely, around the hills and vales like the clouds of the earth. At the risk of being misunderstood, I'd say the pedigree sheep of Scotland and Wales are quite handsome brutes.

There are obvious downsides to being a sheep: it must be pretty boring and people keep nicking your coat. But in many ways life must be utterly idyllic. There's no work to do, you fear no natural predators, and when you eat grass and live in the Brecon Beacons the whole world is your lunch. The equivalent for me would be if every street in London was carpeted with plates of egg and chips.

So I have to ask why so many of them, even now, are standing in the middle of the A4067 between Defynnog and Abercraf. I've tried to work out, using my knowledge of geometry, what percentage of this region of Wales, by area, is road rather than grass. But it's so small I've given up. Proportionally, it's smaller than that irritating bit of lemon grass in a Thai curry.

Standing in the middle of the road really is idiotic behaviour even by the standards of the beasts of the fields, and especially when I'm enjoying the new Vauxhall Monaro VXR. For a sheep, standing in front of one-and-a-half tons of V8 muscle car is a bit like turning up to a jousting tournament in a cardigan.

The Monaro is actually an Australian car, which is strangely relevant as the Aussies have a similar problem with kangaroos. But at least a road-kill kangaroo can be made into what the manager of a Nullabor Roadhouse once described to me as a 'pie-flavoured pie'.

Sheep are unbelievably thick, and when you examine one closely you can see why. They appear to be quite big but, as with Richard Hammond's poodle, there isn't actually very much animal inside that big ball of fluff. And even then, this surprisingly small creature has a disproportionately small head, and hence brain (I once ate a sheep's brain in the Middle East, and I have to say I came away still hungry). Hammond's poodle is merely difficult to shoot at, but a sheep is dangerously witless.

It's not as if they skip about in the road or scamper away in terror. They just sit there looking sheepish as you bear down on them. But if you stop and get out of the car, they run like hell. What does this tell us?

Clearly, we need to deal with the sheep menace, because it's spoiling some of the best driving roads in Britain. So I rang the RSPCA, probably the most powerful organisation in the country, to see what they were going to do about it. The phone was answered by a computer which said 'Press 1 to report a stray animal', but as I was still in Wales I could see that becoming boring.

Eventually, I got through to a preventionist, and her first recommendation was the erection of more fencing. Brilliant. We've never even devised a means of keeping the Scots and the Welsh in, so I can't see us getting very far with their livestock. And here's something else that might surprise animal lovers – according to the RSPCA, there is 'no scientific evidence' that those ultrasonic animal alarm things work. All they mean is that the last thought to pass through the mind of a hedgehog is 'what's that irritating whining noise?'

Apparently, your typical Welsh or Scottish sheep is 'hefted', that is, free to roam. 'They know where they're supposed to be,' said my contact. 'They know where the good grazing is and tend to stay there.'

Well, this is patently untrue. They hide behind rocks in groups and say 'Get ready, lads – here comes one now' before leaping out in front of the big Vozza just as I've snicked it into fourth. I can't stand it. The sheer gormlessness of their faces is putting me off my driving.

The solution is simple. I stopped and spoke to a shepherd in Scotland and he told me that sheep farming is now a completely pointless exercise, with whole fleeces fetching prices that he expressed in pence. So why bother? Get rid of the woolly wastes of space. This is yet more confirmation of something I have suspected for a very long time – that the countryside is not for living or working in, it's just for driving through and admiring.

We can get lamb chops from New Zealand.

A BAD CASE OF MOTORWAY MADNESS

My good friend, the motoring Guru Leonard Setright, once told me that I should only ever ride my motorcycle because I *want* to; never because I *have* to.

To put that another way, the way it appears on the sticker in the back of an Australian tourist's camper van, life is a journey, not a destination. As long as I'm on the motorbike, I'm inclined to agree.

For that reason, I never take my bike on a motorway. Motorways are simply for getting somewhere as quickly as possible, and run contrary to my self-imposed motorcycling ethos. If I found myself riding on a motorway, it would mean I'd selected the wrong vehicle for the trip. I should have taken the car.

But in the last couple of weeks, I've driven hundreds of motorway miles between *Top Gear* filming locations, and yesterday, as I slogged mindlessly along the M11, I suddenly realised that I was *still* in the wrong vehicle. I should have been on the train.

I find motorway driving unbelievably tedious. There is nothing of significance for the driver to do, and yet it demands just enough attentiveness to prevent me from taking a quick nap or doing the *Telegraph* crossword. The Virgin Express makes much more sense.

Yes, I know, you can listen to music in the car. But sometimes the presence of the wireless almost offends me. Has the miracle of motoring palled so quickly that we feel the need to take some minstrels along to entertain us in our torpor? It's tragic.

Apart from anything else, motorways are un-British. Un-European, in fact. In the new world, road-building was a pioneering activity. America grew up with the car and laid the road before it, as a means of conquering a wasteland. Reasonably enough, they made them straight and joined them together in grids.

But in the olde worlde, we have dragged the roads in our wake. They have evolved gradually from faint tracks beaten out by the feet of lonely medieval shepherds and pilgrims to Walsingham. Their character is entirely different.

For example, there is a small riverside path near my house, suitable only for pedestrians and mountain bicyclists. It winds through trees and scrubland and has probably gone unchanged for centuries. Walk down it, and you can imagine how, one day, some commercial or geographical expedient might inspire people to settle next to it. They would shore up the vague track, then they might layer it with gravel to make it more passable in winter. If enough cars started to use it, it would eventually be given a covering of blacktop to become a proper road.

But this process of gradual adaptation would ensure that it always featured the curious left-right kink it has now, there to circumnavigate a boulder or rise in the ground, or perhaps a patch that doesn't drain properly; it would remain as a spiritual link with the ancient wayfarers. And in the age of the car, that is what would make it interesting to drive on.

The best of our car makers build their cars accordingly. Perhaps they simply strive for precise steering or suspension that can absorb all manner of surfaces. Or perhaps it's something more subliminal; just an innate ability to read the road. The British and Italians have generally been best at this. You can sense it equally in a Bentley and a simple Fiat hatchback, in the Alfa 156 or an old Triumph sports car – the impression that the road has inspired the car, rather than that the car has been designed for a road as yet unbuilt.

And how do we celebrate this? By driving on a conveyor belt, where the wit of the engineer and the mystery of heritage are cast aside. At least the Italians have the decency to put some unexpected twists in their autostradas.

Everything about a motorway journey is an affront to even the most vaguely enthusiastic driver. The road is unbending, and so are the staff in the service station. The view is often poor, the food is debased, the din is unrelenting. Even the car seems to be bored because, like the driver, it is bereft of stimulation. The motorway has diverted us from the path of liberty and adventure the car promised and dumped us in a huge automotive gulag.

So I'm giving them up. Other people give up chocolate for Lent, beer for Christmas, or carbohydrates for the holiday season. I'm giving up motorways. I'm foregoing vended sludge for a higher class of brew served in a chipped mug from a roadside caravan. Obviously I'll have to get up much earlier and I'll be spending much more time in the car, negotiating bypasses and driving carefully through the village.

But that's OK. I like driving.

THE JOURNEY'S ONLY JUST STARTED AND I'VE EATEN ALL MY SWEETS

The best thing ever to come out of America, assuming it actually *did* come out of America, is the Maynard's American Hard Gum.

I'm sure you must be familiar with the AHG. It is dome-shaped, brightly coloured, coated with sugar, and probably still stuck in your teeth.

I've been on Hard Gums for well over twenty years now, and a fanciful part of my memory tells me that I bought a bag of them from a petrol station on my very first journey as a newly licensed driver. In all that time I've never been able to suck one all the way to the end. I've often managed to denude one of its sugar, but then I cave in and start chewing.

American Hard Gums do not feature in my life outside of the car: they are completely forgotten once I lock the doors. But this merely heightens the joy of opening the centre console and rediscovering them. Especially on a winter's morning, when they're even harder.

They're the only truly acceptable driver's sweet. Anything involving chocolate is banned from the Bentley because one microscopic speck of the stuff can ruin several acres of hand-crafted and creamy-hued hide. Those boiled sweets in a tin are out as well, because the icing sugar is transferred from the fingertips to all the minor controls and leaves the place looking terribly dusty. In any case, their manufacturer is lying. It says on the lid 'By appointment to HM the Queen', but when I drove Her Maj's Rover P5 a few years ago, they were nowhere to be seen.

No, American Hard Gums it is. They are straightforward, easily managed, explosively tasty and, best of all, completely unpretentious. In a world where the cheese 'n' onion crisp has become the five-cheese and chive flavoured savoury snack item, the American Hard Gum stands as a faintly fluorescent miniature monument to correct on-board eating habits.

Or rather, it did. All of a sudden, they are nowhere to be found. The sweet display at every garage I visit still groans under the weight of chocolate eclairs, fruit pastels, liquorice allsorts, and all the other hollow pretenders to the in-car confectionery crown, but the hook reserved for the hard gums is resolutely empty. There used to come a dreadful day when I would plunge my hand into the cubby behind the handbrake to find only a spoonful of errant sugar nestling in the corner of an otherwise empty bag; that same disappointment has now become a collective issue for the nation's motorists. The Hard Gums are off.

I know I'm not alone. I once bought a second-hand Citroen, and the first time I braked heavily for a roundabout a fossilised AHG rolled out from under the passenger seat to be glimpsed briefly, like a mouse surprised in a pantry, before disappearing again as I backed off. I believe every car has a lost Hard Gum in it somewhere. Hopefully only a yellow one.

I also can't believe they've been withdrawn through lack of demand. By my own conservative calculations, I've eaten well over 100,000 of them in my motoring life. And I'm just one member of the Countrywide AHG Alliance.

I began to suspect a plot when garage attendants claimed not to know what I was talking about. So I decided to ring the makers.

This isn't as easy as it sounds. American Hard Gums are made by Maynards, which is a brand of Cadbury-Trebor-Bassett, which, in turn, is part of Cadbury-Schweppes. They're based in Birmingham, but not Birmingham, Alabama. And in any case, the Hard Gums are made in Sheffield.

I was told I needed to speak to a man called Tony Bilsborough, Cadbury-Trebor-Bassett-Cadbury-Schweppes-

Maynards' head of sweets public relations. He wasn't in, but I did learn some more interesting facts about Hard Gums.

For example, they are 82.4 per cent carbohydrate, which means they can't feature in the Atkins Diet and are therefore completely safe to eat. They contain 0.1 per cent protein, no fat but lots of sugar. This makes them a good energy food, hence their suitability for long motorway journeys late at night. They contain no vitamins, however, so if you ate nothing else you'd get scurvy.

Meanwhile, Mr Bilsborough has contrived to ring me back when I'm not in and leave placatory messages on my answer machine. In the voice of a man who would bite the head off a jelly baby, he is offering to send me a free bag 'if I can find some'. How could he not find some, if he has a factory in Sheffield churning them out in their millions? The evidence is overwhelming – they've been axed.

Well, listen to me, Mr Bilsborough. I don't want a free bag through my door. I want a bag to seduce me as I queue up to pay for my petrol. We motorists are a simple lot. We don't need coffee bars, bonus points, forecourt TV or posh lavatories. We need American Hard Gums. Now.

And if we don't get them, I'm printing your phone number.

PUFF DADDY, A MAN WHO CAN TAKE HIS CAR TO THE LIMIT

Last week, on *Top Gear*, we were talking about bling. I may as well admit that I wasn't entirely sure what everyone was on about.

Bling, as far as I can make out, is about a conspicuous display of wealth. It comes from black popular culture – music, fashion, video and what have you – and manifests itself in very shiny stuff. I expect you knew this already but, because I'm not really very with it, it's all new to me. See? I've said 'with it', and the last person to say that probably died of an LSD-related relapse in the 70s.

Bling can be applied everywhere, it seems: your wrist, your fingers, round your neck and, most apparently, on your car, where you can fit something called 'spinners'. These are separate wheel centres – I'm not going to say 'hub caps' – that rotate independently of the wicked alloys actually holding the tyres on. They might stay stationary while the car is moving, they might continue to rotate when the car is stopped, and, most impressively, some can be made to spin in reverse when the car is moving forwards. So the illusion that always spoiled *Rawhide* on a Saturday morning – ie that when the stagecoach rolled into town its wheels seemed to be going backwards – is now considered the height of on-road sophistication. You can spend £20,000 on a really trick set of spinners.

I have this horrible feeling that I'm not a very bling person. I'm not wealthy enough, and if I was I'd be embarrassed about it, because I'm British. This is why the toffs look so shabby.

Yes, I've got a Bentley, but it's obviously the wrong one. It's a T2, which is pretty much the cheapest Bentley you can buy. The wheels aren't alloy and the tyres aren't big enough. I'm concerned about originality. The stereo is weedy and has a CD of chamber music in it. The glass in the windows is like the stuff in the house – I can see through it, and people can see in, which is all wrong. My watch is smaller than the speedo, and that's wrong too. The T2 is a luxury car for a nervous man with one eye on the wedding hire business.

However, I'm all for bling. In fact, bling could turn out to be the salvation of motoring. Puffy Daddy and his mates may have dubious taste in timepieces, but their attitude to driving is spot on.

Because I've been watching some modern music videos and it seems to me that in Blingland, people drive big, luxurious cars and they drive them slowly. You don't get any Nomex or racing bootees or whiffs of opposite lock or a conversation about understeer. Instead, you'll see some-one sitting too far from the wheel, not holding it properly, and simply enjoying the sensation of chugging about in a really nice motor. That's exactly what I like doing, so as far as I'm concerned – and provided I look beyond the aftermarket snakeskin upholstery – the gangsta rappers are sending out the right message.

It's not a completely new idea, of course. I doubt that the Austin Westminster Car Club, which is based in Budleigh Salterton, does many track days; it would prefer to impress upon you the values of a relaxed ride and an exquisitely trimmed cabin. But they simply don't enjoy the same exposure as Li'l Kim. Here, at last, is a force big enough to confront and defy the motor industry's current obsession with being sporty.

I'm sick to death of 'sporty' cars. Proper sports cars are great, but anything with merely a 'sports' theme is generally the worse for it. This is true of casual wear and pubs, so there's no reason to assume things will be any different for a mildly warmed-up Spanish shopping car. A 'sports' saloon – and they all are these days – is a normal saloon with a worse ride and harder seats. We don't strive to make any other arena of human activity less relaxing, so why do we do it with cars?

I've always maintained that the standard Alfa Romeo 156 is a better car than the over-endowed GTA; that the Rover 75 is nicer to drive than the MG ZT; that a big Mercedes should be left alone, and not given to Brabus to mess up; that ride is ultimately more important than handling. But I've always had difficulty convincing my coevals of this.

What I should have done was waited until they were all watching the Grand Prix and then switched the telly over to MTV. Then they might have got the point.

That, apparently, is what kids are doing these days. We grew up wanting to drive like Alain Prost. But the next generation are growing up wanting to drive like a bloke called Jay Z.

Whoever he is.

NOW IS THE WINTER OF OUR UTTER USELESSNESS

Hitler made a series of tactical blunders but his greatest one was planning to invade Britain in the summer. Had he tried in winter he would have got away with it, because all the Spitfires would have broken down and Dowding would have advised Fighter Command to stay at home. The Vermacht could have strolled into Blighty armed with nothing more than an overcoat and a bag of salt. Instead they had a go at Russia and overlooked that people's fur-hatted capacity for extreme cold.

Every winter it's the same. An icicle forms in Whitehall somewhere, an old bloke's Morris Marina fails to start out in Lower Chodford, and the next day the papers are emblazoned with headlines along the lines of:

BRITAIN LOCKED IN ICE CHAOS

And so it was last week. It was, of course, the coldest Wednesday morning in December since Samuel Pepys began a record in ye diary, or something equally statistically fatuous. But, to be fair, there on the evening news was a picture of a parked car with some snow on its roof. And some football matches were going to be cancelled.

There was more. Somewhere in the North of England – Manchester I think it might have been – industry and commerce had ground to a halt under the cast-iron grip of winter. To prove the point they showed a booted foot tramping desperately across the frozen steppes sunk sole-deep in almost $\frac{1}{8}$th of an inch of light frost.

The trains stopped running, the aeroplanes were all grounded, cars were abandoned everywhere, Halfords was clean out of WD40 and everyone, EVERYONE, had a cold. It's probably because they kept their coats on indoors and couldn't feel the benefit when they went out.

Pathetic. One has to hope no German tourists were watching.

I'm really talking about England here. I've been to Scotland in your frosts and hoars. I've felt the bite of that same wind off the North Sea that rolls mercilessly around your kilts and scuppers any notion of a spot of caber tossing. I have driven all the way to John o' Groats in the snow and seen how the hardy Scot can survive in his draughty crofter's hut, lit by a single spluttering candle and with nought but a tame haggis for company in the eternal night. And by comparison, you're quite good at dealing with it.

But you're still not as good as the Alaskans. I and a photographer have just driven to the northernmost extreme of the US road system, a place where the temperature reached minus thirty and snowflakes the size of marshmallows thudded relentlessly onto the windscreen. Remember that next time some idiot says 'It's too cold to snow'. The Alaskans still get to work in their remote oil pipeline pumping stations. One bloke's sport utility vehicle had got stuck so he was continuing on his snowmobile, commenting as he went that the weather was improving. At least I think that's what he was saying, but I couldn't be sure as ice had formed in his beard. We made it all the way to Prudhoe Bay and back, only got stuck once and retained all our fingers.

All right, so we were in a Land Rover. But it's even colder in the north of Norway, a place we reached in a Lexus LS400 on normal road tyres. Norwegian drivers will survey the weather from three feet within the snorkel of a deeply unfashionable parka and say things like 'So, today we have the snow' before driving off to work at the herring farm. In what? A Jeep? An Audi quattro? No, it's usually a small front-drive hatchback.

Thing is, they know it snows and modify their dress and driving habits accordingly, slithering up the road and holding it sideways through every bend. Occasionally a Norwegian will spin off through a shop window or into a fjord, but overall people get to work and the country prospers.

Yes, they use spiked tyres in the winter and keep snow chains in the boot, but this is a country where the snow can bury a house overnight, not one where the stuff is so unusual that people point at it. It's not as if we have to break out the troika and the balalaikas, we just have to allow longer for our journeys, accelerate more gently and brake a little sooner.

But what happens? We sit in a corner under a blanket with our feet in a bowl of hot water and mustard powder, imagining that to step outside the front door and into the car will spell instant death. Meanwhile, the nation falls apart.

On 27 December I actually heard a policeman on my local radio station advising people to stay indoors until the New Year. My advice is to stop all this feeble snivelling and get out to work.

LEARNING TO DRIVE AT THE CUTTING EDGE

There is a concours classic in my garage. It is a quintessentially British machine – dark green paintwork, red crackle-finish rocker cover and a gleaming chromed petrol cap – and like all the most coveted classics it benefits from what the small ads in *Classic Cars* always call 'lots of history'. It first belonged to some distant relative before being acquired by my parents when I was still a lad. It was later donated to a friend of mine who, at the height of the 80s classics boom, had it fully restored, but when he moved to a small London flat recently he returned it to my care. It is, you will have guessed, the ancestral family Atco and the sort of lawn-mower that made grown men of trembling boys.

The reappearence of the first car I remember, my dad's Morris 8, would move me less. I have not mown a lawn for half my life, yet clasping my hands around the old Atco's rubber grips is as evocative as the scent of freshly cut grass. For I realise now that the lessons learned toiling in its wake have been with me ever since, every time I take the wheel of a car.

For this mere mower was the means by which the sweet mysteries of basic throttle and clutch manipulation – the essentials of driving – were first revealed to me. This was the range-topping twin-clutch model: with the engine speed set by a chrome lever, the first set the blades spinning. The second then engaged the roller and instigated the oft-perilous canter down the long lawn.

Too young to drive, I made the garden my personal proving ground and developed an obsession with the mower that my parents thought unhealthy in an otherwise reasonably balanced teenager. To be a blade of grass in our garden during the early 70s was to lead an ephemeral existence. I would arise during those long, sun-baked school holidays in the sure and certain knowledge that the lawn had grown overnight and head, unbreakfasted, straight for the shed. The four-stroke single barely had time to cool before another tug of the starter sent the local fauna to flight, the flora quaking to its roots and the neighbours lighting bonfires of old tyres in revenge.

There was a hideously tight hairpin round the back of the quince tree. I learned to take it at full throttle, but only by ducking down between the handles and leaning into the bend. Otherwise, a poke in the eye from a branch would see the now-unattended Atco plough relentlessly into the frail hedge or the vegetable plot. Then there was the off-camber strip next to the gravel path. Neglect to correct the drift and the Atco would bite, spinning off and sending up a plume of blade-blunting shrapnel: a strangely familiar scenario and confirmation that Hill and co were tardy about mowing the grass in earlier life.

I learned then that the throttle is the key to control. Too little and the engine would bog down; too much would induce horrific roller-spin or wild oversteer of a sort I later encountered in the Aston Martin Vantage. I have been wary of cruise control ever since that day when I was inspired, inevitably, to set the mower chugging up the garden completely driverless, the idea being to leap the rockery in a single bound and sprint to check its motion in the last yawning instant before it thrashed indiscriminately through the courgettes. But a thumbful of throttle simply made it wheelie dementedly around, making only the occasional deferential nod to its lawn-mowing remit and leaving a series of bald patches among grass, flowers and rhubarb. The problem, I realised, was its exaggerated rear-engined weight bias. Has any novice ever shown the 911RS the respect I instinctively granted it when first I tried one, some fifteen years later?

These days I live in a flat and have no garden of my own, and my parents have long since moved to a smaller house whose apology for a lawn is massacred by a whining Japanese torture instrument on the end of an electrical flex. Yet half a pint of four-star, a few pumps of the carb primer and a tug on the curiously familiar handle would usher in that glittering, golden age of lawn-mowing when the grass was greener and never allowed to grow more than about a millimetre under my feet.

I quickly shut the garage door, recognising a dangerously nostalgic frame of mind. Mint Atco seeks pastures new to tend, lots of history, offers invited. I could develop an unhealthy taste for dark green, vintage British agricultural machinery. Next thing you know I'll have bought an MGB.

THE SOFT UNDERBELLY OF THE DRIVER IS HORRIBLY EXPOSED

Imagine the perfect car journey. Supercar to the South of France? Muscle car across America? Ha! No. I'm reliving it now – a warm summer evening, fine English A-roads and superb music flowing from the highest of fi in the comfort of my kind of car, the latest Rolls-Royce Silver Spur.

I have declared in columns past that I favour a luxurious British motor, and nowhere are those two qualities more apparent than from behind the wheel of what true enthusiasts call a Royce (he was the engineer, you see). Regular readers may now shudder at the prospect of another arcane rant on why a gentleman does not discuss handling; I urge them to read on. This drive caused me to reassess the essential qualities of the marque. Does the Spur corner crisply? *My arse* it does, and I can now say that with authority as on this occasion I was totally, utterly and completely naked.

My good friend Setright,[2] unflagging champion of driving gloves that he is, would no doubt countenance piloting the Spur, if not fully clothed, then in a pair of hand-stitched and unlined kangaroo-skin Y-fronts. But I am no fan of gloves; I like the messages that pass between wheel-rim and palm to go unhindered. So why, I suddenly thought as I bowled through Berkshire, should I tolerate the deadening of any other tactile interface through which the machine communicates with the man? By driving in the buff I would heighten what are normally referred to as those seat-of-the-pants sensations, only this time my pants were in the boot.

Driving a Rolls-Royce in t' niff is not, as it happens, entirely without precedent. The Spirit of Ecstasy, who leans forward from the grille like a vanguard as if scanning the road ahead and who forms, with her upswept arms, a sort of sighting device like the notch on a rifle barrel, by which you

---

[2] Late *Car* columnist.

can train the Spur on some distant point before reeling it in, is, as your mother might say, only just wearing that dress.

Driving in the raw also allowed me neatly to side-step the dilemma I always face when lent one of Crewe's cars: what to wear. Jeans and a T-shirt would only encourage the police in their instinctive conclusion that I had nicked it. A blazer might make me look like a wedding chauffeur. An open-necked shirt would immediately label me as nouveau riche. But in the altogether I am quite obviously just a connoisseur of fine cars.

For how better to appreciate a Rolls-Royce, most poignant and coveted monument to man's earthly and material ambitions, than in the state in which I entered and shall leave the world – with nothing? In any case, a Rolls-Royce simply cannot be enjoyed to the full by anyone with a stitch of kit on. The Wilton is completely wasted on a booted foot and, unless you are a supermodel, the expanse of Connolley's best upholstery will be revealed in its full unblemished glory only in contrast to your own pock-marked hide. Fully rigged, the experience is merely . . . what is the word Rolls-Royce would use? A glance down at my own shrivelled and unworthy form provided the *mot juste* – adequate.

There is a risk, I suppose, that the burghers of Rolls-Royce will take exception to all this. They should not. A car – any car – requires that you form a special relationship with it and, as in all relationships, complete intimacy is achieved only through unashamed nudity. I can only recommend that you try it at least once. Naked, I cemented my spiritual bond with the Silver Spur; bi-level air conditioning ensured that we did not form the corporal one about which the factory's trim department might be a bit worried.

It is only, like so much of the Spur's cabin, natural. I was merely enjoying the car journey of a lifetime: blissfully alone, gloriously uninhibited, driving the way God intended.

A LIFETIME IN THE COMPANY OF JONATHAN PALMER

The line of bollards approached at 80 mph. I heaved on the imaginary brake pedal until only the top of my head remained in contact with the seat. And then we were in. Right, left, right, left, flipped the NSX, and as the oscillations of my flaccid guts went out of phase with those of my torso I think I must have fainted.

Mercifully, oblivion was maintained for the sharp right hander at the end of the straight. I came round with my forehead rattling against glass, perceptions confused as one who wakes from a deep sleep and struggles to untangle the vestige of a dream from the shadowy outlines in a dim room. I was sure I was looking through the side window, yet I was facing the direction of travel. Fiends screeched around my ears and the tunnel of red bollards that rushed towards me seemed like the very mouth of hell.

'The balance of this car is superb,' cackled the devil. No, it was Jonathan Palmer. My senses snapped into line like an NSX after lift-off and I realised we were in the chicane. Beyond that, the exit to the pits. I had to save myself. 'Ho ho, you don't need to convince me,' I said with a knowing chuckle intended to imply that this demonstration of the 'relaunched' NSX would be better devoted to one less informed. Always liked the NSX. Driven it quite a bit. Drove one up here in fact. Love it. May as well just turn off into the pits then. I need to use the lavatory.

I had been loitering at one end of the disused runway that goes on to form the long straight of the Bruntingthorpe track when Palmer pulled up, wearing what I mistook for a hop-in-and-I'll-run-you-back-to-the-pits grin. He had seemed likeable enough earlier on, and in the excitement of the day I had postponed my essential visit to the little room to a dangerous degree.

The pit exit flashed by like a level crossing glimpsed from the window of a runaway train, and for the 100 yards leading up to the sweeping left hander I sat staring open-mouthed at Palmer and pointing idiotically to my left and that rapidly dwindling Portakabin. 'Flat out through here,' he whooped. I had feared as much and set about deploying my visceral differential to apportion muscular effort between controlling my bowels and preventing enforced intimacy with the possessed Palmer. We emerged onto a short straight leading to a right-hander clearly not negotiable at this speed. And there, erected for the benefit of amateurs, was a sign bearing the instruction BRAKE! in a typeface and size to reflect my sentiments exactly.

I was staggered that Palmer hadn't seen it. Annihilation was but a second away and I had to think quickly how to broach the subject of braking but without appearing rude. 'Is this where you would brake for this bend?' I asked, but Palmer, perhaps mistaking my voice for the howl of the Honda V6, said nothing. This was it then. As a lad I'd wanted to be a carpenter. The demons screamed, the car waltzed as if having a look round and then suddenly, miraculously, we were surging out of the bend and my guts were all mixed up with the VTEC valve gear.

There was a brief respite before the tortuous double-apex curve leading to the main straight. *Think.* Engage him in conversation, take his mind off driving. I hit upon the perfect topic. 'What do you think of the standard power steering?' 'Excellent, it was too heavy before.' This was promising. 'It's much more *wieldy* at *low* speed now?'

'Yes.'

The speedo needle climbed and the bile rose. 'But you don't find it too light at high speeds?'. Intended as a subtle hint, my words blossomed into an earnest squeal of impeachment as we slewed through the mother of all compound curves. 'No,' he replied with a pithiness unbecoming of the grand prix commentator. The long straight hoved into view with the hateful slalom in the shimmering, sun-baked distance.

Even I know where the racing line is on a straight bit, and this wasn't it. We were drifting off to the left, heading for another, random scattering of bollards that would be as forgiving as concrete at this speed. Palmer must have blacked out under the cornering forces and his foot was jammed down on the throttle. *I would have to seize the wheel.* Then he spoke. 'Now see how controllable it is, even at 140.'

I really didn't want to insult my host, so it's as well the words *you're mad*, though they formed in my mouth, came out soundlessly owing to the utter airlessness of my lungs. Left, right, right, left – I grasped desperately for a handhold as I added my own wail to the cacophony of tortured tyres and engine, but found that control of all muscles except the one that mattered had been relinquished. My arms flailed uselessly about the cabin and struck something, maybe Palmer, I no longer cared. At 140 mph the sharp right-hander looked like a T-junction: I was dimly aware of a marshal ushering us through with an impatient gesture, like we were boarding a bus, and then . . . nothing.

'How's that?' he asked. I shook my head. The car was stationary and the ticking of the contracting V6 mingled curiously with the twitter of birdsong as if I'd been snatched from the gates of purgatory and plonked squarely in the centre of paradise. 'Terrific, thanks,' I said. He meant the NSX; I was referring to the way he had parked up next to Bruntingthorpe's portable trackside karzi.

ONE DAY I, TOO, WILL BE AN ANCIENT BRITON

If the demographic projections are anything to go by, then by the time I'm old Britain will have only old people in it. This will place a huge burden on the machinery of welfare, healthcare and the factories that produce tartan rugs, but that's nothing compared with the devastating effect a universally ancient population will have on road transport.

I don't like to think of myself as ageist. Time, the subtle thief of youth, has already stolen on its wing my seventh and thirtieth year and life is no longer a, um, boundless and uncharted vista stretching out before me. It is a perfect position from which to observe, without bias, both joyous youth and melancholy old age, and after much careful consideration I've decided that old people can't drive.

I have just completed what must be the most frustrating car journey of my entire life, a twenty-mile trip through town and country and behind a man in a Mini who clearly forgets that he was young once. I've no doubt that he is a loving and entertaining grandpa to someone and that he would be great to share a few pints with over some stories about the blitz, but he seemed about as comfortable behind the wheel of a car as he would be on the dancefloor of an Ibiza nightclub.

Clearly, people born in 1920 were smaller than they are now, probably because they had to eat wood during the war or something. However, the Mini was designed in the properly nourished late 50s, with the result that drivers from an earlier era are forced to look through, rather than over, the steering wheel. This is why old people wear hats in cars. Without the hat poking jauntily above the seat-back, the impression to following motorists would be that the car in front has simply rolled away driverless.

Age had clearly wearied this bloke, as it has so many of his contemporaries. Every time a car came in the opposite direction, he stopped. Every time he approached a car parked at the side of the road he would slow to a crawl and inch his way around it, his head swivelling from nearside to offside and door-mirror to door-mirror so rapidly that it threatened to fall off altogether. The amazing thing is that he was, as I said, driving a Mini yet frustrating my progress in the new Rolls-Royce Corniche, a car so immense that you have to pay the community charge on it.

At traffic lights he revealed himself as one of those annoying people who wait until the lights have long turned to green before selecting first gear and releasing the handbrake. He would then set off with a chirp of front wheelspin before settling down to a steady eighteen mph. Bends in the road clearly terrified him, causing him to slow down so much that I could have stepped from the Rolls and jogged alongside whilst regaling him with some stories about how policemen look so young these days.

I finally lost him at a complex junction a mile from home, where he neatly anticipated the green filter for the turn left lane by mounting the pavement and overtaking two other cars on the inside.

I don't mean to be unkind to the man, but it occurs to me that I have spent years listening to the aged condemn the young motorist while driving around so oblivious to other road users that they are creating a sort of bow wave of terror and last-ditch collision avoidance. Of course he is entitled to go slowly if he wants to, but I cannot excuse the obvious fact that the last time he looked in the rear view mirror he saw one of those new fangled Ford Cortinas. I also wouldn't be surprised if this particular Mini had a bi-focal windscreen.

Why does this worry me? Because I am already aware of the creeping decline in faculties that will eventually see me meandering down the middle of the road like the first driver of the first car. And my ears, too, will stick out alarmingly. I am already beginning to drive too slowly and spend too long at junctions checking that the road is clear. It's not that I'm more careful than I was, it's that I'm less sure.

But I am sure of this. The employment prospects for that future and much diminished generation of youngsters is not as bad as some people make out. When, and if, I attain the great privilege of being really old, one of them will be permanently in my gainful employment. Because he or she is going to be my driver.

I MET MY GRANDPA ON A DARK NIGHT IN THE WEST COUNTRY

Anyone who believes that motoring as an adventure is a thing of the past, and who covets a Caterham 7 or a vintage Bentley to rekindle the old flame, simply needs to go for a drive through Devon.

A glance at page seven of my dog-eared road atlas reveals why. Our motorway system, harbinger and symbol of hope and progress in the 60s, stops with the M5 just inside a county which in so many other ways, too, is locked in an earlier era. One can eat properly in Devon and enjoy tea made correctly, with leaves in a pot. This is reason enough to go there.

There are some fine and beautifully surfaced A roads in Devon, but a little more scrutiny of page seven allowed me to plot a truly epic back-road route for my filial Yuletide visit to the Aged Parents. These are the roads that wend the same way they probably did centuries ago, roads that the motoring age has adapted rather than laid in its all-conquering path; given a lick of tarmac in token fealty to the late twentieth century but not much more. They were certainly never engineered in the way a new road is: the radii are inconsistent, the cambers surprising, and they do not drain properly, or even at all. You will remember that it rained very heavily in late December. For those of you with an interest in typesetting, the roadsigns in rural Devon are writ in something like Indeterminate Extra Light. Also, and for reasons I can't quite explain, at night it's much darker in Devon than in more modern parts of England. I felt I was motoring in a former era.

But then, James May was plying these and similar roads back in the early 40s, when the signposts had been removed altogether and he was forbidden to carry a map lest it should fall into the wrong hands – that is, Jerry's. That was my grandfather who, rejected from front-line military service by dint of his appalling eyesight, elected to drive hopelessly underbraked munitions lorries around the country instead.

Students of oral history will perhaps be appalled that I never recorded in detail the gung-ho lorry-driving tales of the recently departed James May Most Senior. But no matter; I, of course, heard them often enough, so hopefully they are safe for a while yet. The lorry of choice was the eight-wheeled ERF with trailer, powered by a six-cylinder Gardner diesel. In wartime, drivers were obliged to immobilise their charges overnight – usually by removing the cranking handle – lest enemy paratroopers commandeered them. May never bothered, reasoning that the wit, ingenuity and sheer manpower required to start the thing would thwart the invasion more effectively than anything the Home Guard could muster. Each of the six cylinders had to be hand primed before two stout men leapt upon the handle. In winter, when oil was thick and diesel cussed, teams of urchins, including my dad, would be yoked, tug o' war style, to the crank.

Before the days of Granada Services and the Eddie Stobart Fan Club, lorry drivers enjoyed the company of a driver's mate. His job was to manipulate the ratcheted lever of the trailer's separate, cable-operated brakes on downhill sections and then, on uphill ones in winter, grit the road in advance of the ERF's creaking wheels. On one two-day, dock-to-dock run from Bristol to London in winter, my forebear crested a long, icy rise somewhere out in the sticks and, unable to stop the lorry single-handedly on the descent, and reluctant to sacrifice its hard-won momentum on the level, simply continued alone. But then, survivors were not picked up on the Arctic convoys either.

Two days – the ERF was barely able to crack our urban speed limit and even that was vigorously enforced. This was a time when the police didn't even have cars and a rightful sense of sportsmanship governed the business of petty law enforcement; when the police hid behind hedgerows and pursued speeding lorries on foot, blowing whistles. A small pile of HGV permits and papers has come down to me. In 1944 the first James May was fined £1 for speeding. That must have been a lot of money then and it still seems a bit harsh for driving at 25 mph.

Back in 1998, this James May, current incumbent of the family motoring spirit, was fairly lost. Navigation became a matter of studying an inadequate map and stopping at tiny junctions with evocative names like Bozomzeal Cross and scrutinising ancient, awry roadsigns for a clue as to the way to Corkscrew Hill and Hazard. The rain lashed, the blackness closed in, and if I hadn't had a hard top fitted to the MX-5 I'd have lowered the hood, draped myself in a huge oilskin and continued in begoggled and pioneering fashion, attended by the ghost of my forefather.

Six hours after I set off from West London, I arrived on the ancestral doormat. 'Good journey?' asked my father, by way of the traditional family greeting. 'Weather's pretty foul,' I said, adding, before I could stop myself, 'Had a bit of trouble with the dynamo.'

James May the second, who once ran a 1933 Morris Eight, grunted knowingly.

ALL YOU NEED TO KNOW WHEN DRIVING IN FRANCE, PART II

A few weeks ago, I was lamenting this once great nation's obsession with surveys, especially those conducted by boring motor-related industries in a desperate attempt to generate publicity in lazy newspapers and on local radio stations.

In case you missed it, the sort of thing I mean goes something like: women are five times as likely as men to keep a packet of moist cleansing towelettes in the glovebox, according to new research by Damp Dabs. Robert Dullard, managing director and senior vice president (Europe) of Damp Dabs Ltd, says, 'Greasy fingers, from eating chips at motorway service stations, are a driving hazard as they reduce your grip on the steering wheel. Our survey reveals that women have recognised this and usually keep a packet of something like Damp Dabs to hand, but men have been slow to realise the safety benefits of keeping their hands clean whilst on the move.'

Fortunately, I have the perfect antidote to all this nonsense. Every time you come across one of these stories, mentally remove the pivotal phrase 'according to new research' and substitute 'according to some desperate marketing men in a pub'. What Mr Dullard (not his real name) really means is, 'We know women buy Damp Dabs, and we'd really like men to start buying them as well. But we're trying to avoid paying for a proper advert.'

Unfortunately, however, the devious machinery of product and business promotion is one step ahead of me and has already developed a new tactic, which is to send me shameless bids for publicity disguised as selfless advice to the struggling modern motorist.

Only this morning, for example, an organisation called Purple Parking has sent me some handy hints on how to pack the boot of my car before departing for the airport, and whoever wrote them has a first-class degree in waffle from Cobblers College.

'Make sure you understand your car's capacity,' they advise. This is simple. In fact, the rule that applies to the suitcase itself also applies to the boot – if the lid won't shut, you've overdone it. Undeterred, though, Purple Parking continues to push the outside of the envelope of the bleedin' obvious with a guide to successful unpacking: 'Do not drop luggage on anyone's foot'. This is insultingly facile and as a result I'm not going to dignify Purple Parking (which offers facilities at nineteen UK airports, it says here) with a free plug.

But while their advice is merely fatuous, that from Europ Assistance (who describe themselves as 'the pioneer of continental motoring breakdown for UK motorists') is actually wrong. Admittedly, many of the suggestions contained in their top tips for driving in France are sensible if rather achingly apparent: carry a reflective warning triangle, remember to drive on the right, beware of highwaymen, and so on. But then they recommend that you should 'drive slower than you do at home, as it will give you more time to react to the unfamiliar'.

Of course, there are many features of France that will be unfamiliar to the alleged three million drivers who, this summer, will depart the modern and progressive bosom of Britain to holiday there in squatty lavatory medieval misery: people in berets, vast tracts of farmland producing nothing, the smell of cheese, Frenchmen driving two inches from your rear bumper, people trying to park in spaces two feet shorter than the car they're in, the curious absence of any reference to the 2012 Olympic games, and so forth. But these are not reasons to slow down. They are an incitement to put your foot down and get to Italy as soon as possible.

Apart from anything else, one of the few pleasures of motoring in France is the freedom to drive like hell through their countryside. Why do you imagine that the annual 24 Heurs du Mans is so popular with British car and motor-cycle enthusiasts? It's not the prospect of the race at the Sarthe that excites them, it's the race there. Even coevals of mine who purport to advocate lower national speed limits for the UK admit to driving like lunatics through France; and reasonably enough, since they're abroad and therefore it doesn't matter.

The French do it, after all, and driving slowly is hazard-ous, since you increase the risk that a Peugeot 206 driven to within a few degrees of meltdown will end up in your boot.

Still, if you do have a shunt, Europ Assistance (who claim to have recovered over 220,000 UK motorists from conti-nental motoring calamities over the last 35 years) does at last offer some sensible advice. 'Because you are a foreigner, you are more likely to be blamed for it. So it is more crucial than ever not to admit liability,' they suggest. 'Nor to apologise.'

Good work.

LOST IN THE INFINITE SPACE OF A HOTEL LOBBY

As regular readers will know, I've spent much of the last few months and quite a lot of money learning to fly a light aircraft. I wish to boast that it's going terribly well so far.

I can take the aeroplane off the ground, climb, descend, turn, glide, operate all the knobs and levers and even put it back on the deck in such a way that the next student will be able to use it. Provided that I pass the medical, my instructor says I can go solo, and if I manage that successfully I'll be sent off on my own to practise my navigation. And that, finally, is when the whole thing will go a bit pear-shaped.

Navigation is a real problem for me. Not map-reading, which is purely logical: I can read a map. I'm quite good at spatial skills and can construct highly convoluted Scalextric circuits for the delight of children. But for some reason I have a clinical inability to store any sort of map in my head, and of that intuitive sense of direction that most people have – how many times they've turned right or left – I am completely bereft.

I know other people with a poor sense of direction, and they try to pass it off as an endearing characteristic. Mine is so bad it makes me look utterly stupid. I check in to quaint country-house hotels with a sense of trepidation, because the Elizabethans and Victorians were fond of multiple staircases and meandering corridors that mean it will take me hours to find my way to breakfast. I like modern tower-block hotels, where you can only go up and down in the lift and left or right when you get out. It's pathetic.

So I've now bought one of those portable Navman sat-nav devices. It can be fitted to any of my cars in seconds, and the digital harridan inside it knows the way from anywhere to anywhere else. It's quite brilliant.

But I do have one highly personal criticism of sat-nav in general. Because it works in the minutiae of junctions and corners, it is like looking at a map through the hole in the centre of a bog-roll. It relieves me of the need to develop a mental picture of the general arrangement of Britain's towns, cities and major geographical features, and as a result I have even less of one than ever before.

And let's be honest here: one is never truly *lost* in the car. Cars move only in two dimensions; you can drive only where the road goes, even if it's the wrong one; there are signposts on the ground and if all else fails it is theoretically possible to stop and ask someone.

Now let us return to the cockpit of Piper Warrior G-WARU at 1,300 feet somewhere over Surrey, en route to White Waltham airfield for the rejoin, circuit and landing. If the Warrior were fitted with a black box recorder, the transcript might read something like:

INSTRUCTOR: There's Bracknell on the right and point Whisky on the left, so if you look ahead you'll see a square wood, and about ten degrees to the left and a bit beyond that is a row of poplar trees. Follow the line of those and you see a triangular field. The airfield is just beyond that and you can see runway 29. Got it?
STUDENT: No.

For a start I know sod-all about trees, and how am I supposed to identify bloody Bracknell from up here? It looks exactly the same as Reading. It's hopeless. You know those coffee-table picture books with titles such as *Britain from the Air*? That's exactly what it looks like. Try finding your way around using one of those.

Still, at least my time aloft has left me with this uplifting observation concerning our road-atlas view of Britain. A glance through the AA book in your car would suggest that the place is horribly built up and cluttered; that the poet Larkin may have been right when he said, 'All that remains for us will be concrete and tyres'.

But he was wrong. The map you know is deceitful, is horribly distorted by roads drawn such that in reality they'd be half a mile wide. At 500 feet the small ones are already difficult to discern. By 2,000 feet even the major ones are revealed to be no more than scratches on the earth. At 3,000 feet Bracknell (or it might be Maidenhead) is little more than a smudge, and by a mere 4,000 feet this island looks like the world as Adam would have known it, an endless and uninterrupted vista of arcadia rolling away on all sides. It is beautiful, unspoilt and, above all else, green.

Unfortunately, so is the airfield.

ALL YOU NEED TO KNOW WHEN DRIVING IN FRANCE, PART III

If there's one thing I like it's a nice broad, sweeping generalisation or a solid, dependable hackneyed old stereotype.

I especially like national stereotypes. They're harmless, fun, and probably a lot more accurate than we care to believe. I don't care if Italians think I buy condoms in packs of twelve so that I'll have one for every month of the year, because in return it leaves me free to assume that all Italian men are mummy's boys and that a hand grenade goes off in the belly of an Italian woman the instant she gets married. The Australians think we're all whiners. Great. It means I can continue to regard them as backward because they think the height of sophistication is to cook your dinner outside over a bonfire. In Britain you do that because you're a tramp.

And then there are the French, one of my favourite targets for a big broadside of ill-informed prejudice. Blah blah the war blah blah garlic blah blah berets moan moan communist tendencies drone drone referendum grumble grumble cheese smells funny.

Of course France isn't all bad. Jeremy, who secretly likes to think he *is* French, always maintains that food in humdrum French restaurants is better than it is in the equivalent establishments in England. And, much as I like to disagree with him as a simple matter of principle, on this occasion I may have to acknowledge that he could conceivably be right, technically.

We've just returned from a short motoring holiday we took together in France, and I have to say we ate simply and excellently; even in a remote hotel, the British equivalent of which was no doubt serving something described as 'oven-roast', as if you could do it any other way. The French really do seem to be more discerning in the matter of salad leaves and take more pleasure in serving them to you. It pains me deeply to have to concede a point from the Main Land to those subsidised sheep-burning bastards, but there it is.

Mind you, they pay rather less respect to the opposite end of the alimentary system. The karzi I used in a roadside café appeared to have been untouched since Richard the Lionheart passed through. Great food but crap bogs, which means no matter how exquisite your *croque monsieur* is, it's going to end badly.

What really bothers me about France, though, is this. If you go there in a nice car, it will be destroyed and you will be killed. Simple as that. The French drive like *les lunatiques* half an inch (12.7 mm) from your rear bumper and there isn't a single car in gay Paris without a stoved-in panel on it somewhere. They're mad.

Or are they? On our Boy's Own hols I was driving a Ferrari F430, which is not a car you'd normally want to take onto the Arc de Triomphe so-called 'roundabout'. You may as well park up and go round it with a mallet, just to get it over with. Jeremy was in the Ford GT, and to make matters worse for him it was his own car (for this week, anyway), and he was in the position of being asked to scrap it already. Meanwhile, Hammond was in a Pagani Zonda that he had on loan from a man we knew simply as 'Mr Corleone', so you can imagine how he felt about all this.

And yet, after a few laps of the famous monument to Europe's second-best general we emerged from one of its twelve exits completely unscathed. A man in a Renault Megane actually stopped at one point and gestured to me to go before him. I immediately concluded that this must be some British bloke in a hire car.

But then again, on one of the few occasions when I got out of the Fezza I found myself standing at a zebra crossing, and the next thing I knew a woman in an immaculate

Citroen Xantia had stopped and beckoned me across. In the good old days a French zebra crossing meant 'cross if you dare, English scum', but now it seems to work just like one of ours. And she was definitely French, because she was wearing difficult spectacles with ludicrous pointy bits, and only French women do that.

Something strange has happened. I've actually been to France several times over the last month, and on each visit I've been struck not for once by a car but by how politely the French are driving these days. Imagine my frustration. In the old days I could sit down to dinner in the brasserie and rant all night about how dreadful French driving is. Now I'm forced to whitter on about how marvellous the bread is, just like everyone else.

That's not the end. I've been to Spain recently too, and something similar is going on there. Not so long ago driving through Spain was a simple matter of marvelling at the quality of the roads we've paid for and swerving around corpses and the wreckage of old Seats, but now it's all 'after you, hombre' and using the indicators. Again, I managed to convince myself that this was the work of British people who keep a small hatchback at their holiday villa, but the fact is that at least one of the drivers I encountered was wearing one of those Don Juan de Marco waistcoats, so he was definitely a Spaniard.

This is terrible. I want to be able to rant with a clear conscience about their fish-thieving, but it's difficult while they're all being so bloody nice to me. I hope to God I never have to go to the Ukraine again. If they turn out to be driving around in a dignified and courteous manner instead of hooning around in broken Volgas while whacked on hooky vodka, my life will be ruined.

Whatever next? Germans driving slowly? Welsh people driving quickly? The Belgians being funny? At this rate I'm going to have to go all the way to the States to find something to gripe about. It's a bit like waking up one day to discover that Jeremy has become a reasonable, balanced sort of bloke and Richard Hammond doesn't want a fight. For a week or so it would be great, but then I'd want them to go back to being an arse and a pain in the arse respectively and calling me Captain Slow all the time, because I actually prefer them that way.

Forget the constitution, or the currency, or the rules on competition. Just stop this appalling driving reasonableness. It's destroying Europe.

Vive la différence, as they say in Italy.

THE OWNERSHIP ISSUE

RACING TO THE CAR-CARE COUNTER IMPROVES THE BREED

There's something spooky going on at the man/machine interface. This much I have discovered during a week spent with the Alfa Romeo 156 V6.

Now here is a car I genuinely desire and one I would actually buy if I had a real job. It is a *proper motor car*, with a burbly engine endowed with a respectable number of cylinders, lovely responses, and all that. My only complaint was that the V6 had too many gears. Otherwise it was seductive, powerful, a thing of beauty and a joy.

But not for ever. After a few days I drove it in the rain and the nose got all covered in skite. Late braking dulled the inner recesses of those wonderful alloys with dust. A recalcitrant bag of my favourite American Hard Gums went off in the cockpit and spattered the instrument panel with sugar, and I'd smoked a small and rather poor quality cigar in it while stuck in a jam. That new-car smell was gone and the Alfa had already crested the brow of the long incline that leads inevitably to the scrapyard. It wasn't half as good any more.

So I went to the garage and took down the brimful box of car-care products sent to me over the years in the hope of editorial appraisal. I began on the inside with Armor-all plastics restorer and Halfords interior air freshener, before moving to the outside and applying Turtlewax car shampoo with my Holts jumbo car sponge. I returned the alloys to their former splendour with Wonder Wheels and then ran my coarse hands over the Alfa's beautiful body to apply Mer Liquid Wax to the paintwork and a dab of Autosol to those fabulous door handles, finishing off by buffing the whole with Autoglym lint-free polishing cloth.

And do you know what? Performance, ride, roadholding and, especially, refinement were all immediately improved as a result. Tosh! I hear you cry. And yet, so help me, 'tis true.

I couldn't explain it, but maybe some of the country's eminent academic minds could. I knocked up a quick fax and fired it off to the professors of engineering and psychology at a few universities, asking the simple question *Why does my car run better after I've cleaned it?* As a control measure I also sent it to Setright who, almost by return of fax, submitted a treatise of medieval density on the subject. But from the ivory towers of academia – nothing. Either they'd gone straight to the lab to start experimenting or they were preparing a lecture on wasting people's time.

My follow-up calls were no more encouraging. Two profs had disappeared entirely, while another relayed the message 'no idea whatsoever'. I tried Susan Iverson, head of psychology at Oxford, and did at least succeed in speaking to the professor, something I never quite managed during my own years of study. 'Not my area of psychology at all,' she told me. 'I'm a neuroscientist. I don't clean my car. My husband does it for me.' Psychological bullying, perhaps? 'No, idleness.' A two-one for honesty, then, but no help in my insatiable quest for knowledge.

It was then I realised that I was asking the wrong sort of people. Intellectuals probably *talk* about cleaning their cars, or attempt to place car-cleaning in a socio-economic context, but they don't *do* it. A cacky car is a professorial badge of office, like ridiculous hair and pipe-smoking. Anyway, I worded the question wrongly. It should have been *My car runs better after I've cleaned it . . . discuss.*

Disheartened, I turned to Setright, who suggested that the phenomenon I had observed was a purely psychological one caused by the release of chemicals into the brain during the exertion of the cleaning process. But I wasn't totally convinced, not least because this came from a man whose idea of excercise is to stand up whilst smoking. Certainly, cleaning affects the mood of the driver, but I reckon the mood of the driver affects the performance of the car, too. Still think it's tosh? I am indebted to Professor DW Clarke, head of engineering science at Oxford, for the following anecdotal evidence.

During the 30s British engineers conducted exhaustive experiments on railway locomotives in an attempt to improve efficiency, but without conclusive results. Eventually, they plucked an in-service engine at random and painted its funnel blue. This had no bearing whatsoever on its performance, but it did have the effect of telling the hitherto unwitting driver and fireman that they were under some sort of official scrutiny.

A one per cent improvement in efficiency was recorded.

IF YOU LIKE TO GAMBLE, BABY, I'M YOUR MAN

A year and a half ago, I bought a 1980 Bentley T2 as one of those 'Bentley-for-Mondeo-money' experiments that car journalists are always writing about but never actually try for real.

Well, I did. So I can now tell you, from a position of absolute authority, that it's bollocks.

The Bentley is a lovely old bus and I'm keeping it. Nothing much compares to an early morning swoop along a tree-lined B road, Parry or Britten or some other domestic composer slotted in the CD player, Crewe's finest ironmongery wafting me from crest to crest through the very landscape that inspired the sounds in the aromatic cabin. Now That's What I Call England.

However. I'm rather tired of having to flog off my childhood treasures on eBay just to pay for the fuel, and the simple fact is that although the value of the car may have fallen to Mondeo levels, the cost of maintenance is going the other way. Because it is built entirely of perishable materials it has to live in a garage, and the nearest one long enough is nearly eight miles away. That meant even more expenditure on a folding bicycle.

Finally, I'm heartily sick of people climbing into the back and then exclaiming, as if no one has ever thought of it before, 'Ha-ha! Home, James!' I'm not going without stair carpet so that people can treat me like a factotum.

So it was time for another car. Something for local use. If I were driving to Scotland then I would sell some more Dinky toys and take the T2, but the rest of the time I would make do with something smaller and more frugal.

And a car I've always fancied is the Range Rover Classic, the Vogue SE model with air suspension. I know this sounds a bit daft but if you're used to a T2 the Rangey counts as a handy hatchback. You might think 20 mpg is a bit excessive, but when you're used to 12 or 13 it represents a 50 per cent improvement. Range Rover it was, then.

Remarkably, Richard Hammond had come up with exactly the same idea. He'd even found one to go and look at – a one-owner 1993 car belonging to a man he knew, with a full history, and for a frankly incredible £4,000. 'Let me know what it's like,' I said. 'If it's good, I'll have it.'

Well, that evening he rang me, and from the uninterrupted tirade of yokel exclamations I gleaned that it was a 'minter'. So good, in fact, that he'd taken the money he was supposed to be using to mend his house and bought it for himself.

You can imagine how annoyed I was. A mint Range Rover for £4,000 didn't sound like the sort of thing that would come up very often. 'Bring it round,' I suggested. 'I'd like to see what you really get for that sort of money.'

'No,' he said.

Instead, he challenged me to a game of Car Poker. Here's how it works. Hammond would bring his Range Rover round to my house, but only once I'd bought the same model at the same price. I had to pay to 'see' him, if you like. The best car would win, and there was a curry on the table.

Well, I still wanted one so off I went, scouring the country, Hammond ringing me up every few hours to bait me with more news of how good his was. I soon learned that £4,000 Range Rovers vary enormously: some were positively whiffy, some were quite nice. But it was difficult to know how good Hammond's really was. He could just be bluffing.

Eventually I found myself at a small dealership called Impulse Motors looking at something very promising. It was the same year as Hammond's, the mileage was the same to within 5,000, and it too had a full history. This one was silver with grey leather, which I thought looked very urban and sophisticated; Hammond's, I knew, was green with brown trim, as befitting his hurdy-gurdy rural lifestyle amongst the mud and peasants of Gloucestershire.

The upper tailgate was a bit rusty, but then, they always are on old Range Rovers. Aren't they? The front bumper had been dinged as well, but so what? There were a few minor scuffs on the leather but as Hammond's car had seen the same amount of use, his must have them as well. Or would it? He said it was 'mint' but then, his idea of mint might not be mine. Hammond has taxed and insured things that the rest of us would arrange to have removed by the council. By 'mint' he might merely mean 'complete', which would be a first for him.

Still, Car Poker provided an interesting new spin on the hackneyed language of haggling. 'I can't give you four and a half for this,' I said to the slightly baffled salesman. 'Hammond only paid four grand, and his is mint.'

'What?' he said, 'Better than this one?'

'Don't know. I haven't seen it yet.'

Eventually, I parted with £4,100 and came home quaking with nervous excitement. It wasn't just that £4,000 is not the sort of sum I find in the pocket of an old jacket, or that the insurance was a bit steep, or that I'd landed myself with another complex old British barge to attend to. There was also the fear that I might have to buy Hamster a bhuna. That would really hurt.

We met in the *Top Gear* car park. I couldn't believe it. He had bought the only Range Rover in Britain with an unblemished tailgate. He had a patch of corrosion on a wheel-arch, but I had my knackered front bumper. Mine was a more interesting colour scheme, but his smelled better. It was close, but then he played the card that Motorhead warned us about: the joker.

An LPG conversion. His was bi-fuel. I know the duty might go up in a few months' time and the whole thing will look like a waste of boot space, but until then he's running his car at two-thirds the money it's costing me. So my first expense as a Range Rover owner, even before I'd put any petrol in it, was a £25 invoice from the Light of Nepal.

But what a great way to go car-buying. Left to my own devices, I might have become impatient and bought on impulse. Instead, the spectre of Hammond stuffing his smug face at my expense forced me to search harder and haggle more aggressively. So Richard Hammond has the best £4,000 Range Rover in Britain, but so what? Car Poker has given me the second-best one instead of the bag of bolts I usually buy.

It's time for someone more enterprising than me to set up a Car Poker website to bring together people from across the country searching for the same car at the same price. At the end of the game, they can meet in a mutually convenient Little Chef to compare purchases.

Loser buys the Olympic Breakfast.

LAND ROVER – AS OLD AS THE HILLS. THAT'S HOW IT SHOULD BE.

Never let it be said that I'm not a true motoring enthusiast. I've just spent a week in a Land Rover Defender 90 which, the more learned among you will know, is available only as a diesel. So that's army transport powered by the evil genius of Dr Rudolf, and I've driven it exclusively around London.

It's a 90-inch job with a station wagon body plus some Lara Croft extras such as tread plates in unnecessary places. I'm constantly flabbergasted by it. It's basic design is older than my house, and you have to live in a pretty new house before you can say that of any other car currently in production. It doesn't just hark from a time before computer-aided design, it seems to be rooted in an age prior to the invention of the mathematical instruments set we used for designing cars in the back of our maths books. The shape was obviously worked out using some pieces of folded cardboard, and the last time I saw hinges like the ones on the Defender's back door they were on the smokebox of a locomotive in the Science Museum.

Oh sure, one or two cosmetic bits have been added over the decades. Lights and what have you, and a new plastic radiator grille. But as soon as you drive in to a few things on your 'expeditions' these will all fall off, and then you'll be back with the Wilkes brothers' farm biffabout of 1948.

I love it. It's definitely a chap's car. A woman would look ridiculous in it because you'd know she must have more sense. I, on the other hand, am very happy bouncing around the capital, parking up and then standing on the bonnet just because I can. You may like to arrive in style; I like to arrive with an arse like a farmer's face. Just how utilitarian is this thing? Well, there's a flap just under the windscreen, running the full width of the vehicle, which can be opened with a crude lever from inside. You open this if the engine's not quite noisy enough for you. When you take it to the jet wash, you can do the inside too.

However. Yesterday, something bothered me about the Landie. At first I thought it was the centre console, which features all sorts of things that don't belong in a Defender – electric window switches, seat heater switches, heated screen switches and a radio. Fitting these to a Defender is like carpeting a shed.

But it wasn't just that. The real problem was that it was just too new. Somehow, a Land Rover is only truly acceptable when it's old, and ideally given to you by your dad. I can't really explain why, but it's a bit like shotguns and wristwatches. Or money.

Now my colleague Hammond – he has a Land Rover that is cresting the peak of elegant decay. It's a 110 V8 with canvas and sticks (as Hammond would say. He means it's got a removable and roll-upable fabric roof supported by a collapsible steel frame. And it usually does).

It's black, but where the paint is flaking off you can see that it used to be red and the property of the Post Office. From a distance it looks quite tidy, but up close vegetation can be observed taking root at any sharp included angle. Anything not absolutely essential simply isn't there any more, and several things that were once part of the engine are now in the passenger's footwell.

It really is quite magnificent and it has got me thinking. Soon, the Defender will go out of production and England will be ruined unless something is done about it. Fortunately, I have a plan.

The other day, I had dinner with a man in his late 40s at his home. At the end of the meal he took out a bottle of rather fine but deeply obscure single malt whisky. Well, it turned out to be his own. His father had bought a whole barrel of the stuff, freshly distilled, in the 70s and then left it in a hut somewhere in Scotland to age. This bloke hadn't so much drunk his inheritance as inherited his drink.

Let's face it – no one has ever walked into a bar and asked for a nice young Scotch. The older the better, and that's only possible if our forebears take the trouble to put the stuff aside for us. It requires a disciplined and far-sighted society, which is probably why we don't have eighteen-year-old Greek Ouzo.

Land Rover – officially at any rate – can't actually build an old car, so it's up to us to lay a few down while we've still got the chance.

This requires thought. Whisky needs an old Sherry barrel from the Peninsula. Balsamic vinegar, to take another highly coveted example, has to pass through a succession of barrels of various woods if it is to achieve the right flavour, and that can take twelve years. I quite like the idea of a barn-matured Defender. My experiences with the things suggest that two decades in the back of a cow shed should be just about right. That would give it a good nose.

On the other hand, those with a hardier palate might prefer a field-aged model, parked in a meadow with the windows half open to ensure a good mossy finish in 2025.

Come to think of it, this scheme would work rather well for the new Bentley Continental GT as well. It's a great car now but, rather like that cheap French grog that most of its first owners will drive off to collect once a year, rather nouveau. Half a lifetime in the car park of the Savoy, doors left unlocked so the odd pissed toff can sleep in it, should make it more pukka than a Rembrandt with your relations in it.

Sadly, my own father never did this for me, and I don't have any children of my own. So – had a son recently? Put his name down for a posh school or a golf club if you must, but for God's sake put him down for a Defender.

TOOLS – TWO OF THEM

Not for the first time this year, a massive row has broken out in my garage. The last one was between me and my good mate Colin over whether or not my old Moto Guzzi should be restored to show-winning condition, or just left as we found it after twenty years in the back of a damp shed.

I won that one, and the old Guzzi cruises the streets of London resplendent in that unmistakable fresh-from-shed patina.

Still, that was a civilised and reasoned debate conducted over oily mugs of tea in a manly fashion. This one was a right barney worthy of a couple of fishwives and lowered the tone of the neighbourhood even further than the bike does. It concerns tools.

A bit of background first. Colin and I are an invincible pairing when it comes to DIY car and motorcycle maintenance. Colin has owned far more old knockers than I have and has been riding motorcycles since before he was legally entitled to. Every one he has owned – and it's over thirty – has been stripped and rebuilt with his own hands and usually in the kitchen. His mind is one big exploded diagram.

On the downside, however, he is apt to go at a new repair project like panic mechanic, sometimes with the sort of dire consequences that end up advertised in the back of a classics magazine as 'unfinished project'.

I, on the other hand, have nothing like as much knowledge to draw on but am blessed with a legendary pedantry when it comes to practical tasks. I will look at a job for hours on end, making sketches, taking photographs and even having a long lie down before so much as opening the big red toolbox. It's boring, I know, but in my defence I have so far avoided committing the miracle of reassembling a car or motorcycle using fewer components than the original manufacturer did.

So the combination of Colin's experience and my patience can, frankly, achieve almost anything – even a new bypass hose on the old Mini (Mini sufferers will know what I mean). And all we had to do was rebuild the front forks of the old Guzzi. But then, as the fashionable expression goes, it all kicked off.

Should a tool go back in its tray in the box as soon as you've finished using it, or should it go on the floor near the bike on the grounds that it will be needed again in a minute? I'm a back-in-the-box man myself, but Colin favours a big clear-up at the end of the session. Does it matter? Oh yes.

Here's a typical scenario. I'm holding a fiendishly complex throttle linkage together, against the pressure of the spring that operates it, with one hand. With the other, I need the 8 mm ring spanner to secure it. If I had it last, it will be within reach of the other arm, in the second drawer, between the 7 mm and 9 mm spanners. But if Colin had it last it could be anywhere, and twisting to locate it can see the whole assembly fly apart with a cartoon 'boing' noise, never to be seen again.

But if Colin's doing this job, he will position himself to retrieve the spanner from the floor, where he left it, with his free hand. Except that I used it last, and it's back in the toolbox. Boing.

It doesn't sound like a big issue but believe me, it will end with pistons at dawn. You cannot imagine the rage that flares up in my breast when I open the spanner drawer and I am mocked by a space where the 8mm should be. You are not, I hope, familiar with the language Colin employs when he balances the spanner on a footrest to take a swig of tea and I pick it up and put it away.

In my defence, I point out that surgeons keep their instruments in order on a tray, so that they are not left inside the patient. And spanners do look remarkably like parts of the bike. Colin points out that if Ferrari kept putting their tools away, they would lose every F1 race in the pits.

I'd like some real mechanics to write in and tell us who is right, to settle this once and for all. It's important. It's the sort of thing Japanese production engineers spend months studying, in the hope of liberating another 50p profit from a Toyota through improved assembly line efficiency.

But before you write in, consider the strange noise that was coming from under the bonnet of my Range Rover the other day. It sounded like a little end at the very least. Or maybe a big and expensive gearbox problem. A real death rattle. I stopped, lifted the bonnet and stared at the engine very hard. And guess what it was?

Someone had left a screwdriver in there.

GOT A GARAGE? YOU'LL NEED SOMEWHERE TO PARK THE CAR.

Here's something you probably didn't know about my good friend and TV colleague Dr Jeremy Clarkson. Next to his house, he has built a sizeable garage. And do you know what he keeps in it? His car. What an inordinately dull man.

No such slavish adherence to convention in the May household. I was in the garage only this morning, looking for my training shoes. This may strike you as rather odd, and I have to say it struck me as rather odd too. Until, that is, I conducted a quick inventory of the brick out-house.

I'll say straight away that there is no car in it. There are my motorcycles, but if I'm honest they are only in there because I can't manoeuvre them through the dog-legged front door into the kitchen. Then there are the bicycles. I counted seven in all, which is alarming in itself and even more alarming when you consider that some of them aren't even mine.

Beyond this, though, the garage is little more than a shrine to abandoned fads, neurosis and plain idleness. Here, for example, is my 60s Avon inflatable boat and the 2 hp Yamaha outboard that goes with it. And next to that, the ancient Seagull outboard I bought from eBay at considerable expense in the interests of greater authenticity. When I'm dead someone will no-doubt flog the Yamaha on eBay to someone who bought a rubber boat in 2004 and who wants it to 'look right', and so it will continue unto eternity in other garages.

The Black and Decker Workmate, some taps, a bollard, a painting-by-numbers a friend did for me ('I'll be hanging it on the wall,' I told him, without specifying which one). Still, I know I'm not alone.

Let's imagine you went out today and spent £2,000 on a new sideboard. My bet is that you'd bring it home and put it in your house. Yet I know people who spend upwards of £20,000 on a car and then leave it on the street, even though they have garages. This seems to be a peculiarly British condition. German and American garages contain a car and nothing else. But British garages are full of junk.

It's all the same junk as well. I dare say there is some owner-specific junk out there – Stephen Bayley probably has a few spare objets d'art in his garage; Attenborough, some left-over dinosaur bones. But they'll all have several half-empty tins of paint.

It is a simple fact of life that one cannot buy the right amount of paint. There's always some left, and a deep-rooted social convention says it goes at the back of the garage. There is some paint in mine from a previous house. Dulux, I am convinced, makes no profit at all from the paint on your walls. The mark-up takes the form of millions of gallons of magnolia abandoned in urban garages.

An why do we keep 'spare' bathroom tiles? Do we imagine that we might lose some of the ones glued to the walls around the bath?

One explanation for this nation's misappropriation of garage space can be found in ancient history. At some time in the 30s, someone in authority decided that this new motoring malarkey would never get any bigger than the Austin Seven, designed a garage to suit and enshrined its dimensions in British Standards. Moving on to 2004, the Volvo estate ends up in the street and the old mattresses are in the garage, since it's much more conveniently situated than the municipal dump. Clarkson can get his car in there only because he had the foresight to add thirty per cent to the architect's drawings.

But this does not explain the actions of my other TV colleague, Richard Hammond. Recently, he demolished his old garage and built a much bigger one. I visited him between the demise of the old building and the completion of the new one and there, on the drive, freshly removed from the condemned garage, was a large pile of what is often referred to as 'mancrap' – a plastic canoe, a guitar amplifier, some hi-fi separates, paint, spare bathroom tiles and his Land Rover. I assumed this was all going to landfill, but no. On completion of the new garage it was all moved back in.

The reason is simple. Garage junk is a great comfort. As men, we can retreat into the fetid gloom, confront the debris of our failures – the rusting exercise bicycle, the woodcarving tools, the tennis racquets – and come to terms with them. The British garage is a place of exorcism, and pulling the wobbly aluminium door shut is an act loaded with symbolism. It could never be wasted on a car.

I found the trainers, by the way. They were behind the camping equipment, next to the useful offcuts of wood. Then I threw them away.

It's a start.

WHAT THE MOTOR INDUSTRY COULD LEARN
FROM MUSIC

Of all the ailments that can afflict a car, by far the worst is an irritating squeak or rattle. A catastrophic breakdown is a one-off, instant hit of pure misery but one that, once over, can be forgotten. A breakdown is a bit like a swift beating; a squeak is a constant torment of a sort probably used on political prisoners.

They are also notoriously difficult to cure. There are cars that rolled off the production line with a squeaky rear parcel shelf, squeaked for a lifetime despite the efforts of technicians to put things right at every service, and doubtless gave a last defiant squeak of badly fitted plastic as the jaws of the crusher closed around them. Still, in a car at least you can turn the radio up.

Now imagine, if you can, a similar problem with a baby grand piano. Some weeks ago I bought a brand new one in an effort to rekindle my musical past. Recently, it developed an irritating buzz from the B-flat above middle C. This may not sound like much, but just as the squeaky shelf has a disproportionate impact on the pleasure of every car journey, so the buzzing B-flat is ruining an otherwise highly agreeable instrument. It's also spoiling what I rather optimistically like to think of as my artistry.

In fact, I have now developed a pathological aversion to the offending key, so my neighbours are probably wondering why Scott Joplin's *Maple Leaf Rag* has no B-flat in it any more.

And the problem is nothing apparent. Obviously, the first thing I did with my new grand, even before I'd played a note, was to put a framed picture of my mother on top of the lid. I've removed that, in case mum was rattling around a bit; I've also removed the metronome, the faux Art-Deco lamp and – shameful, this – my crash helmet. But it's still there. I've played with a mate lying underneath the piano and another with his head inside it, but still the source of the resonance eludes us. I've checked everything for tightness and I've had the thing in bits searching for a rogue screw or washer, but to no avail. When one of those mates told me to 'just play louder' (i.e. turn the radio up) I finally lost my rag and told him to *ff* off.

This is serious. The composer John Cage once defined music as 'organised sound', which was a good way of explaining much that he did. But even Cage couldn't pass off my B-flat because the buzz simply isn't in the score. If I'm going to have a buzzing B-flat, I may as well set a digital watch to go off during the slow movement.

Look – I know this is the motoring column and not the music page, but there are some interesting parallels here. I bought a Japanese piano because it was notably better value than a European one. It also came with a corking warranty. There was no part exchange as the piano showroom didn't deal in broken motorcycles, but by paying cash I was able to negotiate a substantial discount. So far, this could be a new Yaris.

But from here on, the piano-buying experience shames the car-buying one. 'This sort of thing is common in older pianos,' said Steve from the piano shop, when I rang him with my complaint. As much is true of parcel shelves. 'But it shouldn't happen in a new one.' Quite.

Clearly, he couldn't tell me that they all do that, sir. I've just listened to Andras Schiff play Bach's entire *Wohltemperierte Klavier* on CD. Music types will know that these 48 preludes and fugues were written to show that a keyboard instrument tuned to 'equal temperament' would sound right in any key. Today, they also serve to demonstrate that Herr Schiff is not having to endure a single extraneous vibration from anywhere in his Joanna. So neither should I.

'I'll have someone round in half an hour,' said Steve. I bet you don't get that sort of service from your Toyota dealer.

Well, that someone is here as I write – a piano technician, a member of one of the most secretive social groups on earth, with their curiously unfamiliar tools, their earnest, ear-straining expressions, and their urge to play *Strangers In The Night* in order to test their work.

In fact, he's been here for several hours, pulling the thing apart, hammering bits, twisting things, sticking pins in felt, grovelling on the floor and banging his head on the soundboard to create something that clearly isn't music because it obviously wasn't organised. And all for what is, in the end, just an annoying little rattle.

If he can fix this, I'm putting him in touch with some car manufacturers.

DANGEROUS DOGS MAUL MAN'S CAR-BUYING BUDGET

On the whole, I rather like animals. I like the elegance of cats, the nobility of horses, the endearingly witless resignation of cattle and, perhaps best of all, the comedy-eared inquisitiveness of donkeys. My favourite dog is a Border Collie, for its intelligence and loyalty. Yet something about dog ownership has always made me uneasy.

And now I know why. It turns out, according to a story in last week's Daily Bellylaugh, that a dog, over its projected lifetime, costs the same as a new BMW 3-series. I think I know where my money would go.

Exactly which 3-series I ended up with would depend, of course, on the precise type of mutt I'd left whimpering, unrescued, in the Battersea Dogs' Home. But we can now get a pretty good idea of where dog lovers stand in the hierarchy of BMW non-ownership following the annual 'Cost of a Dog' report by Churchill Insurance (logo: a dog). Even a Jack Russell, a small dog but one that resolutely refuses to die, can knock you back £17,500, and that will get you into a basic 3-series Compact. A friend of mine had one of these (a Jack Russell, I mean) and it used to sit in the fireplace. Even when the fire was lit. That was the little bastard's way of telling his master that he'd be behind the wheel of a rusty MkIII Escort for some time to come yet.

At the other end of the scale, Great Dane owners can scoop up mountains of dog pooh in plastic bags and shovel vast quantities of cheap pie-filling into the mouths of their insatiable pedigree chums in the certain knowledge that Fido will never be sticking his head out of the back window of the lovely 3.0-litre coupe model.

I can't quite decide whether these findings reveal dogs to be very expensive or cars to be surprisingly cheap. What I am sure of, however, is that it's time for a Japanese electronics engineer to design some sort of dogbot that really is just for Christmas, and which, along with all the other battery powered novelties you bought for your kids, expires mercifully on Boxing Day afternoon. After that you can just stick your own face in your visitors' crotches and save yourself a fortune.

This peerless piece of research also finally explains why my colleague Richard Hammond's car collection is so pitiable. The man has four dogs, which puts him about £80,000 in arrears even before he's so much as bought a 'spares or repair' basket case off eBay. They're eating him out of some very nice cars. I only have a cat, which eats whatever I'm trying to eat, and I've just acquired a couple of goldfish, which I calculate will cost no more than £6 a year to run. So over their projected lifetime they'll have set me back about £1.50.

I suspect that Hammond takes a dog-owner's approach to car ownership, which is why his garage is full of old Land Rovers. When these become too smelly and incontinent for the family home, they can be given away to remote farms: exactly what you'd do with a clapped-out Labrador.

Meanwhile, and on the subject of dogs, I've used the vast wealth I've accrued through not having one to buy an old Jaguar. I hadn't been planning to buy a Jag but I just couldn't resist it when the vendor opened the garage and I saw its loveable face peering at me imploringly out of the gloom.

It's the rare but rather beautiful XJ6 Coupé model, a mustard-coloured example from 1976. It's in excellent condition, the only problems being a couple of small rust bubbles on the rear wings and that the control for the driver's electrically operated door mirror is broken. But I could hardly knock the man down on the latter fault, since I broke it on the test drive.

Now that the cheque is cashed and my name is on the V5 registration document, I could safely reveal how much I paid for this car without the risk of someone pointing out to the former owner that I was effectively about to steal it. But that would be ungentlemanly, so let's just say it cost about the same as a Highland Terrier that gets run over after three years; or, to put it another way, a couple of hundred king-sized bags of Winalot, a tartan dog-coat, worming and a castration. Yet here's the Jaguar, at about 140 dog-years old, still going strong.

It is, in fact, the most elderly of my fleet of faithful old friends, all of which seem to be working perfectly. But do you know what?

I get the horrible feeling that, any day now, one of them is going to bite me really badly.

THE BUSY MAN'S GUIDE TO BUYING AN OLD PORSCHE

In my life so far I have owned three homes, and in each case I bought the first one I looked at.

This may seem like a pretty blasé approach to the most onerous financial and administrative commitment a chap can ever undertake, but to me it makes complete sense. All homes these days have internal lavatories and the electric light, so why waste time and effort looking at several that are going to be essentially the same? Providing everything works, the roof isn't falling off and it doesn't back on to a railway marshalling yard, you may as well move straight in and save yourself the misery of tramping around the neighbourhood with a witless estate agent.

People tell me that buying a house is life's most stressful event, but I have to say I've always found it incredibly easy. It's not really that different from buying a pair of trousers. If they fit, you have them, thereby freeing up your mind for something far more important, such as buying a sports car. This, obviously, is much harder.

I've been thinking for a while now that it's about time I had something a bit more fruity than the Bentley and the old Range Rover. These two remain utterly peerless – the Bentley peerlessly pompous and the Range Rover peerlessly practical – and I'm keeping them. But I'm now 42, and if I didn't want a sports car I wouldn't be a proper middle-aged bloke.

And I mean a proper, powerful and slightly hairy sports car, not a 'sporty' saloon or hatchback, which is something else altogether; namely a normal saloon or hatchback with horrid trim and a terrible ride.

But anything new that I fancied – Boxster, BMW Z4, Honda S2000 – was too expensive, so I found myself driven once again into the fateful embrace of *Classic Cars* magazine with a budget of £16,000. And after a while, I discovered a problem.

It is this. If you decide you want, or need, to live in Lower Chodford, you look for a house in Lower Chodford. They're all going to be pretty close together. But if, as I did, you decide a 70s BMW 3.0CSL would be an interesting car, you might have to travel hundreds of miles to look at one. Travelling five miles to look at a house with an avocado bathroom suite is merely annoying, but driving 200 miles to look at a BMW that turns out to be an absolute snotter is infuriating. After a few such trips, I decided that I just couldn't be bothered to find a good CSL.

It's the same with old Alfa Giulliettas and Triumph Stags. What misty-eyed classics enthusiasts describe as 'totally original' is what estate agents describe as 'benefiting from many period features', ie knackered.

I realised I would have to apply my house-buying technique to buying a sports car, and that meant buying an old Porsche 911. The 911 has always been well made, there are plenty of them around, and there are independent dealerships specialising in them. In fact, there was one not fifteen miles from me, called 911 Virgin. You could look them up on the interweb at www.911virgin.com, but for God's sake don't add an 's' to 'virgin' or you will end up on a deviant site featuring nudity and skateboards but no cars.

I fancied an 80s 3.2-litre Carrera without any body kit or big spoilers. They had one of those in a discreet silver colour with blue leather seats, in super condition and with a rock solid service history. So I went to look at it. It was good, so I had that one.

Obviously, there was a bit of unseemly talk of money involved. This dealership offers two prices on each car. One is a trade price, at which you buy the car as seen with no come back. This was £14,995. The other is the retail price, which includes a full service, rectification of any faults, and then a three month warranty covering everything including normal wear and tear to clutch, gearbox and what have you. Then the price was £16,995. Although I'm not strictly a 911 virgin, since I've driven dozens, I've never gone all the way and lived with one, so in the end I lost my bottle and went for the second option. But after the usual arms-folded forecourt stand-off I'd negotiated some new inner rear wheel arches and knocked them down by £1,250.

Essentially, then, I'd walked in to a 911 shop and bought the first 911 I saw. Easy. A few weeks ago I had to buy the ingredients for a Thai stir-fry. It took a lot longer.

HOW PORSCHE RUINED THE 911, BY A BLOKE WITH AN OLD ONE

Welcome, readers, to the most eagerly anticipated comparative road test of the last twenty years; a definitive distillation of two decades of inconclusive ramblings by some of the most boring people on earth. This test liberates one of the greatest debates of our times from the stagnant arena of the local pub and addresses it anew in the fresh, balanced and beer-free environment of the East Sussex lanes. Yes, folks, it's Porsche 911 Carrera versus Porsche 911 Carrera.

On the left, in red the base-model 911 for 2005, the Carrera. On the right, in silver, emerging from the early morning fog just as the gleaming brand Excalibur was held aloft in the mists of Avalon by the mystic, wonderful, samite-cloaked hand of Nimue, my own car, the 1985 base-model Carrera. So – which is best?

Twenty years separate the two cars, and twenty-three years separate my car from the original. Pedants could even make a case for a direct link with the VW of the 30s, since the guts of the Beetle were used to create the post-war Porsche 356 and the basic layout of that car inspired the 911. But already we have arrived at the nub of what put me off buying a 911 for so long – namely, that 911 owners can be rather nerdy.

The 85 car is significant since in many ways it represents the last hoorah of the original, being essentially the same shape but mechanically improved and endowed with more bhp yet still bereft of power steering or any other driver aids that later served to banish the 911's reputation as a widow-maker. Shame.

(And here is another curious link I have just come up with. The Beetle, the true forefather of this car, was designed by Porsche but is generally regarded to have been loosely stolen from an air-cooled, rear-engined prototype built by Hans Ludwinka of the Czech company Tatra. Ludwinka also designed a rear-engined V8 monster called the T87, which was very popular with German officers until Hitler forbade its use, such was the toll its fearsome handling traits exacted on his senior staff. They had to make do with the Beetle-based Kubelwagen instead. A generation later, the ghost of the betrayed Ludwinka emerged in Porsche's 911, and promptly started lobbing the owners into ditches again.)

Sorry. Anyway, parking these two cars side-by-side demolishes any notion that the 911 is some sort of automotive immutable. Place any recent 911 next to its immediate predecessor and you will get a sense of its gentle evolution. But separate them by four generations, as we do here, and you can see that there is not a single component in common between the unadulterated 80s thoroughbred and the lumpen approximation claiming to be its rightful heir. Even the badge is different. The only constant in this equation is that the engine is still in the back, but that's at best just bloodymindedness and at worst a pathetic attempt by Porsche to fake a spiritual relationship between the new 911 and the sort of car they produced in their heyday (which, in case you hadn't worked it out, was 1985).

Toyota has attempted a similar stunt with the Corolla, claiming that the same car has been around for half a lifetime. No one is fooled there, and I'm not fooled here. Just because the new 911 feels, in essence, like the old one, and the engine makes the same sort of noise and vibrates the viscera in the same way, and the front end still feels as lively as it ever did, doesn't mean there is any significant similarity between the peerless silver car and the tawdry appliance on the left spoiling your view of it.

Yes, they've mimicked the instrument layout of the old car in the new, but again, I'm not going to be swayed by mere tinsel. The heating and ventilation works perfectly in the 2005 car, revealing that Porsche in fact has no sense of its recent heritage.

Of course, the later car is *technically* faster and more stable, and has superior brakes, but these are hardly the attributes the connoisseur demands of a true sports car. We want the unalloyed pleasure of bowling along a B road, seemingly propelled by just a handful of moving parts thumping away in the back somewhere, and at the mercy of wonky stoppers if it starts raining. We don't want to feel that we can climb into a Porsche and emerge unruffled in Monte Carlo. The best 911 ever, then, is the 1985 3.2 Carrera.

Curiously, I've just been reading *C20th Cars* by Hilton Holloway and Martin Buckley. It features a smattering of 911 variants, but not the one representing the apex of its development, which was the 3.2 Carrera of 1985. This book is therefore rubbish and not recommended.[3]

---

[3] It's actually rather good.

I PUT MY MONEY WHERE MY MOUSE IS AND BOUGHT A PUP

A couple of years ago, I accidentally enrolled on a twelve-month fitness plan at a local gym. I blame the drink.

I was at a charity auction in my local pub, in aid of cancer relief. Some framed prints and candlelit dinners for two had already gone at well over market value when the landlord approached me. 'Could you kick off the bidding for the gym membership with a decent figure?' he asked. 'Only it's a really valuable prize and they've been very generous. Just to get it going, you know.'

Well, there were a lot of wealthy and, I thought, very charitable people in the pub that night. Fat, too. And I knew that the health and vitality plan would cost about £1,000 over the counter. So when Lot twenty came round I stuck up my hand and bid £700, only to be rewarded with a deafening silence broken only by the evocative fall of the gavel.

I have a bit of a history of this sort of thing. I've also accidentally joined a book club and accidentally bought a pension. Only a few weeks ago a man from this newspaper rang and asked if I'd like to take part in the Thundersprint motorcycle race meeting in Northwich next month. I said no, but it must have been another trick question because next thing I knew I had a competition licence and an entry number. I'm even less accomplished at performance motor-cycling than I am at the bench press.

But all this pales into insignificance after this morning, when I awoke to discover that I'd accidentally bought a car.

This time I blame a combination of the drink and the goading of a TV colleague whose name I won't reveal other than to say it begins with R and ends with ichard Hammond. It was late, we'd been to the BAFTAs (which we didn't win) and we were surfing eBay searching for – can't quite remember why, but perhaps he can play one – a double bass.

In case you don't understand eBay, as I obviously didn't, here's how it works. Anybody can advertise anything lying around their loft/garage/spare room, and other members of the 'eBay Community' can bid for it over a fixed time. At the end, the highest bid wins the goods, and the deal appears to be legally binding. Everything imaginable is on eBay (except a double bass) – it's like a sort of virtual car boot sale, only some of the cars are for sale as well.

It's a Mini.

I've been whittering on for weeks about owning an old Mini, and here was one – a 1275 special with trick alloys and a comedy paint job. With encouragement from my whooping colleague I entered a bid slightly higher than the current one and – you can probably guess this by now – nobody else did. So now it's mine.

And it really is mine. Unless it is not as described – i.e. it's not a Mini at all but a nest of tables – I have to cough up and take it away.

Still, it looks terrific in the pictures. Really tasty Minilite wheels, some cracking extra spotlights on the grille, flared arches, chequered roof – the lot. Trouble is, I can't help noticing that everything on eBay looks terrific. The pictures are only a few inches square and they're displayed on a computer. Just to reassure myself I went outside with my own digital camera and took a picture of my neighbour's truly shabby old Toyota. It has several dents, matt paint-work and very poor wheels and tyres. Then I downloaded it onto my computer. That looked terrific as well.

I would just like to confirm that this escapade breaks all the golden rules of car buying; runs contrary to everything Quentin Wilson (God rest his bones) ever taught me. I know it has tax and an MoT, and the vendor gave a very fulsome description of all its irrelevant features, such as the K&N

air filter, the polished window winders, the CD player and the chromed exhaust embelisher. But I haven't checked it for sill rust, the condition of the sub-frame mountings, the engine tie-bar bushes, cam-chain rattle, bald front tyres and everything else doubtlessly on the *Practical Classics* Mini-buyer's checklist. How could I? I have, in effect, only ever seen it down a telephone line.

And even then there was something I didn't notice. I live in West London, and somewhere on the eBay page, quite close to the most emphatic declaration that the buyer must collect, was confirmation that the car lives near Buxton.

Remember, readers – don't drink and drive. Don't drink and buy, either.

LOVE FOR SALE – PRICE INCLUDES LEXUS

Wine comes in at the mouth
And love comes in at the eye;
That's all we shall know for truth
Before we grow old and die.
I lift my glass to my mouth
I look at you, and I sigh.

Yeats wasn't a bad poet but some of the ideas expressed in this *Drinking Song* of 1912 are looking a bit dated. For a start, these days he wouldn't be drinking wine but some pseudo Irish ale served up in a fatuous themed pub. And anyway, this is the digital age, when love comes in at the ear.

Love, which, as ever, has crept in unexpected to find me wanting. I had climbed unwittingly aboard the Lexus LS400 and set its satellite navigation system for some tiny street at the opposite end of town. I would arrive a smitten man.

For no sooner had I pulled away than a voice – a voice so plaintive, so laden with melancholy – rose from the dark depths of the dashboard and coursed straight for my heart: *at the traffic lights, turn right.* I felt at once the strange churning in the bowels familiar to any teenager who has stood outside the door of the nice girl with the stern father.

This is not my first encounter with digital woman. The Royal Bank of Scotland's telephone banking system, by which I can attempt to shore up my pathetic finances via the telephone's buttons in response to computerised prompts, features one such. At the end of every transaction she says: *thank you for calling Royal Bank Direct Banking. Goodbye.* And, though she is just some solid state representation of the warm flesh and heaving bosom of genuine womanhood, I am somehow never able to put the phone down until she has finished talking. But that is merely me being prudish, and anyway she is a bearer of bad news, her voice dropping almost an octave as she adds the word 'over-drawn'. In the Lexus, I am run clean through with Cupid's goldenmost arrow.

On the face of it, this swooning, fragile flower was a poor choice for the car. I am only a man, so after a while decided I knew better which way to go and started ignoring her instructions – to love, after all, is one thing; to obey, quite another. My fifth-year tutor, Crooksy, would have been more appropriate – then, at the third transgression, the device would say *by God, May, you will regret this*. Yet even as I erred the fair voice came, human in my faithless ear, patient and – this is the 90s – *supportive*, and I knew then what Yeats meant when he said that all men's hearts must burn and beat. All this, remember, from satellite navigation, the one device designed to release me from torment. Now I am lost without her.

Hang on, you're saying, it isn't really a woman, it's just a chip. But that's like my mate's grandmother listening to some music on the radio and then saying 'That must be a record. No one can play the piano that well.' The real woman is alive somewhere; the process by which she was transferred to the computer might be called 'sampling', but I prefer to think of it as imprisonment. Just as, in the early days of photography, superstitious people believed that the picture plucked the soul from the subject, so too do I believe that the LS400 has locked this hapless maiden in a world of woe and despair, with no one to take her to the pub or buy her chips.

And as I drove, she cried out to me with what might seem to you like directions – *at the junction, straight ahead* – but always ending with a wistful cadence that this suitor correctly interpreted as *save me*. And so I shall. I shall find my Rapunzel of the facia and release her from her misery, and she me from mine.

Assuming, of course, that she's prepared to let her hair down.

DEAD CARS AND DEAD POETS – DEAD SCARY BUSINESS

One day I am going to be flattened by a car as I negotiate the complex crossing en route to that bedrock and pillar of the local community, Mr Patel's newsagents. The roads converge from three directions via blind bends but I never press the button for the green man; I just time my leap with ever greater brinksmanship, poking the grim reaper with a pointy stick and then legging it. The combined rules of statistics and laws of sod say that eventually I will get it wrong and the circulation of *Scotland on Sunday* will diminish by one.

So be it. In the midst of life, we are in death, even when all we wanted was a paper and a Cornish pasty. And one day, too, my beloved Jaguar will be in a scrapyard.

I've spent a bit of time in a scrapyard this week and the experience has put me in a sober mood. Always has, ever since, as a fresh-faced eighteen-year-old, I walked into my local breaker's yard in search of the missing boot badge for my otherwise complete MkI Vauxhall Cavalier. Wandering around the heaps of carcasses I came across one of my dad's old cars.

Imagine, if you possibly can, the effect of this on the sensitive youth, to whom life was still an infinite vista without horizon stretching away in front. There was my dad's Cortina MkIII GXL, already shaken off the mortal coil. I prised the badge off that instead and still have it, and it still invokes that dread realisation of mortality.

Like any self-respecting shaggy-headed sixth-former, I read a lot of poetry back then and couldn't help noticing that the young Tennyson must have come across one of his dad's old cars in a scrapyard, too:

All things must die.
Spring will come never more.
Oh! Vanity!
Death waits at the door.

All this came back to me as I loitered in a scrapyard in Italy during a photoshoot for the new Vauxhall Astra Coupé. From a distance an Italian scrapyard looks little different from the roads in the centre of any Italian city, but close up you have to admit that even the Italians can't pile 'em up six high and upside-down. Here, then, was a poignant moment revisited, like Brideshead.

The scrappy and his chums crowded around the Astra, as if amazed that a car can actually look like that. I suppose it was a dangerous place to take it, given his widely evinced urge to pull its doors off and drop an old Peugeot on its roof. Yet once, every car here was like our Vauxhall: shiny in every nook and cranny and an object of unalloyed joy to its new owner. Even the Fiat Strada.

The scrap merchant is nothing more than the undertaker of the motor industry, and I can't help feeling that dead cars should be afforded a little more respect. To think that one day the likes of his dog will piss all over the hide of the Sovereign's back seat and his lad will chuck stones at its windscreen in an idle moment. One day, the silken bores of the Jag's V8 will, like the exposed cylinders of this beheaded Alfa engine, be stopped with rust. They could at least persuade some flowers to grow between the corpses.

I realise that these are not terribly original thoughts and I apologise for being soppy, but I just cannot stand in a scrapyard looking at the flattened shell of a Citroen CX Pallas without imagining the day when, at the other end of its life, a smoothy in a sharp suit handed the keys to its new owner, someone who at that point probably did not envisage the grease-caked vandal now going at it with a hammer. I must also pause and ask myself why it is that scrap merchants never seem to have a full complement of teeth. And I cannot poke around the barely recognisable hulk of a very early Cinquecento without noting that it still has one serviceable door handle that an enthusiastic restorer, somewhere, is looking for.

It's all so sad, but perhaps it's also healthy. The 70s Lancia whose battered bonnet I sat on was once a highly aspirational item, yet a short time reveals it to have been an earthly conceit, and the earth is where it is about to return. The Jaguar is, in the end, only a car; and I am only a man.

Bit of a bugger, isn't it? Now I suggest we all go out for a nice drive while the going's still good.

EVERYTHING YOU NEED TO KNOW ABOUT THE *****-***** *****

A car launch is generally a pretty salutary experience and the aspect of this job that makes it the envy of boys in short trousers. And quite a few men in suits, if they're honest. You get an interesting location, often abroad, a good lunch, a souvenir corporate biro (of which I have a stunning collection) and, best of all, an interesting new car to drive around a pre-ordained and varied route.

There is, however, one invariable that serves to ruin every car launch I've ever been on and which can cast a grey cloud even over two days in Barcelona driving a new Seat. It is the equivalent, in my job, of your boss saying, 'Have a nice holiday, Binks; I've got some bad news for you when you return.' It is that I have to write about the car when I get home.

But not this time. I've just spent three days in sunny southern California driving a very interesting and expensive motor and you are about to learn the square root of nought about it, because I am not allowed to tell you anything. And that is actually the fault of *Scotland on Sunday*, because this page counts as 'the motoring section of a national newspaper'.

Country Life, meanwhile, is classified as a 'lifestyle title', and as it happens I am its motoring correspondent. Therefore, I was invited by ***** to what marketing people would call the 'lifestyle reveal' of its new *****, provided I undertook to write about it only there and not here, because the official launch to the motoring press will be later in the year.

So that's that then. I was going to ring the editor and tell him that I wouldn't be doing a column this week, because I was in the curious position of having had my work banned before I'd even written it, a scheme of things that would have saved DH Lawrence a great deal of trouble as he could have gone to the pub instead of wasting his evenings writing *Lady Chatterly's Lover*. But then I had a thought.

The idea behind the event was to give us a taste of the sort of lifestyle enjoyed by the prospective ***** owner; or, as *****-*****'s PR man put it, 'You can appreciate it only if you put yourselves in the frame of mind of the kind of person who'll be buying the *****-***** *****. So if I describe the lifestyle correctly, you should be able to guess the identity of the car. There's a corporate gift for the first correct answer.

Palm Springs is pretty warm even in January, which meant we could cruise around with the hood down all day. But before that, I had a sauna and sat in a hot spa with a naked Dutch journalist. Then a huge bloke called Bud or Buzz or something took me into a small room and gave me what the Givenchy Spa brochure described as a therapeutic massage but which felt remarkably like being beaten up by a football coach. Then I had lunch. Then I had another lunch, because it was there, and then I went for a drive in the new *****.

It would have been highly appropriate if *****-***** could have arranged for each correspondent to role-play a famous anecdote involving a ***** owner, in which an elderly man is attempting to reverse his ***** into a tight space. As he selects gear, a young blade on a motorbike swerves behind him and occupies the space, removing his helmet and saying, 'You've gotta be young to do that, mister.' The ***** driver thinks for a moment and then backs in anyway, smashing up the back of the car and completely destroying the motorcycle. He then climbs out and says, 'You've gotta be rich to do that, son.' And you have, because this car costs a whopping £*******.

Being a ***** owner is great. The next day I spent a happy hour attempting to blow things to bits with a

Holland & Holland 12-bore that cost half as much as my house. That night there were at least two bottles of Krug each for dinner, after which one noted member of the fourth estate hijacked an electric golfing trolley and attempted to drive it into the swimming pool for the full lifestyle effect. But, not being a proper motoring journalist, he was unable to find reverse and in any case, a member of staff correctly identified him as an upstart, not a true ***** owner and told him to get the **** out of it. Attempts to feign decadence by drinking Krug and smoking Bolivars in the back of the new ***** were also proscribed by a gently perspiring PR man, lest a few stains and holes in the Connolly and Wilton should betray our poor breeding. This is a clue, by the way.

As Rolf Harris would say, can you guess what it is yet? Send your answer to *Scotland on Sunday*, and remember to mark your envelope 'Lifestyle Section Competition'. First correct one opened wins my Rolls-Royce lapel badge.

Woops . . .

ALUMINIUM COMMODITY COLLAPSES WITH DIRE RESULTS

It's often said that kids these days don't walk anywhere. It's true. They're driven to school, driven to Cub Scouts and driven to the shops to buy new trainers. When they're not being driven somewhere they're inside playing Nintendo, and on those rare occasions when they have to get somewhere by their own efforts they do it on one of those folding scooters.

Unless you've been detained by Her Majesty for the past six months you will know about these things, because every child in Christendom has one. I've just heard the rattle of one going past the window. It is my honest belief that the current generation of infants will never be able to walk upright in the accepted *Homo Erectus* fashion, as they seem to be plucked straight from the breast and installed on a scooter without bothering with the intermediate crawling and toddling stages.

A while back someone gave me a Micro Scooter as a gift, and the cast and welded aluminium marvel, made in China at an ex-works price of about 50p and sold on your high street for almost £100, has got me thinking. I know this is meant to be a motoring column, but the real issue is personal transport and scooting may just have something going for it.

For uphill stretches, scooting is obviously inefficient. Too much uphill work will give the rider an Olympian left leg and a horribly shrivelled right one. On the level, though, it's about twice as quick and half as much effort as walking, and on the vaguest of descents it should offer that most elusive of commodities, something for nothing.

What's more, the Micro is so ridiculously lightweight and commendably collapsible that it's no burden at all to carry on the ascents. On the face of it, then, the Micro would appear to be as significant an evolutionary step as coming down from the trees. It gives you freewheeling feet, which is exactly what anyone living at the top of a mountain has always wanted.

Inspired, I unfolded the Micro and went for a familiarisation run in a nearby car park, where I was immediately challenged by a small girl similarly equipped and barely out of the womb to a race around the perimeter. She thrashed the pants off me and disappeared laughing into the rising sun.

Undeterred, I set off for the airport, hand baggage over one shoulder and Micro over the other, hoping to scoot my way nonchalantly to the departure gate. This is where I would prove the efficacy of the scooter in any situation where tediously expansive flat surfaces have to be traversed in a hurry – airports, warehouses, the decks of supertankers, the Millennium Dome.

Instead, I learned the first rule of scooting, which is never to scoot in a turn. If you scoot in a turn the weight is transferred away from the front wheel, causing it to 'step out'. Having skipped sideways the front wheel then grips anew and the rider is introduced to the type of crash most feared by motorcyclists – the 'high side'.

For a split second the complex cornering forces no longer resolve and the rider is catapulted over the top of the vehicle. Anyone entering Terminal 1 check-in at that moment would have been amazed to see a man flying without the aid of an aeroplane.

More experimentation needed. So I set off one morning on the Micro to Postman Patel's corner emporium, the local answer to local supply demands, served in this instance by the new local transport solution, to pick up my copy of *Scotland on Sunday* and a Cornish pasty.

Sadly, the Micro's wheels are so small that an uneven paving slab that would go unnoticed to a pedestrian becomes an insuperable obstacle to the scooterist. For the second time I found myself continuing my journey sans scooter, trying desperately not to knee myself in the face and wondering if I'd ever be able to have any children.

It's not quite right. The running gear is badly specified, the low bars force you into an absurd sporting posture and there's no radio. In the end, it's only a toy and an unsuitable one at that. Having failed to master the Micro, I've now decided that they should be banned.

I mean, yesterday I was wandering around the supermarket when, at the junction of spices and tinned fruit, a small boy who should have been at home watching videos rounded the corner at high speed and scooted straight into me. What sort of society is it that thinks it's acceptable for children to scoot round a supermarket?

I realised I would have to fill that yawning post-collision silence during which the brat would decide if there's was anything to be gained by crying. 'I've got one of those,' I said. 'They're crap.'

He ran off blubbing to his mother. I expect he'll want a new bike now.

ASK ME AN HONEST QUESTION – EVERYONE ELSE DOES

Ever since childhood I have had to live with a rare and incurable handicap known as ask-me face.

I cannot venture more than a few miles into central London before a Japanese tourist asks me where Buckingham Parace is. If I loiter in one position between the shelves of B&Q for more than a minute, someone will enquire as to the whereabouts of the four-by-two timber. 'Do I look like an assistant?' I always ask, and they always say 'Yes'.

The other day I checked in to a smart country hotel in the North of England, and as I stood at reception a man – a Scotsman, as it happens – approached me to see about getting some ironing done. When I posed for the picture at the top of this column I made a point of pulling a particularly sour expression, for fear that readers might otherwise write in to ask me for directions to Lower Chodford.

Frankly, this has always held me back in life. For while my contemporaries were forging ahead with glittering careers in banking and telecommunications, I was out on the pavement talking to someone with a clipboard. Now imagine what happens when I install my ask-me countenance in an ask-me car.

The car in question is one I have alluded to before and which I have been driving to an extent out of all proportion to my chances of ever owning one. It is the new Rolls-Royce Corniche, a car about which I have written so many articles that I could now afford to buy a set of lambswool rugs for one.

I now understand why, when an example of the old Corniche comes up for sale, it only ever has about 5000 miles on the clock. I thought it was because they were cherished cars that had been used only for very special occasions; I now realise that no owner has ever managed a journey of more than ten miles before being beaten back by the mob.

I also know why a Corniche is, according to its makers, invariably bought as one of a stable of cars. As a means of meeting the local community the Corniche is a more effective medium than a church fête, but if you actually want to get anywhere you're much better off in the Mercedes.

I realise, as well, why Corniche owners always have a second home in the wilds of northern Scotland or the remote regions of southern Spain. They don't actually need the house, they simply need somewhere to drive the Rolls without interruption.

In the same way that a trawler captain cannot escape the flock of seagulls that attends his working hours, I cannot drive this car without being pursued by a slavering pack of rabid inquisitors: What's it like then, mister?; I bet that costs a few bob to fill up; there's not much room in the back, is there?; mind you, this is a German car now; how much will one of these set me back then, eh?

Comedians, too: I thought I told you to bring it round tomorrow; I'll swap you for the wife; hello, dad; aye oop, the butler's here; how d'you like yer new VW?; I thought I told you to wait in the car, Jeeves; and so on.

I was off to see some distant mates in the Royce and when they asked me what time I'd be arriving, I had to say: 'Well, in the Jag it would be about five o'clock, but I'm in the Corniche today so you'd better add another hour to allow for people wanting to look at the engine.' One woman actually asked if I'd drive her home in it 'to give my husband a shock.' And it was my own mother.

At first I felt that I should share with other members of the downtrodden proletariat the great privilege I was enjoying. But after an American tourist asked if I'd take his photograph with the Corniche, I started to think more in terms of bugger off, the lot of you.

I've already told three people and I'm not even out of the car park yet. And I already knew the one about the English Rolls-Royce driver who works for Cunard in shipping and an Irish petrol-pump attendant who says he works forkin' 'ard in his garage but only has a Ford Fiesta.

Given my own Caribbean island, the Corniche would be a wonderful car to own. As it is, life's just too short. I don't know when I'll be driving it again but if, when I do, you happen to see me, don't even ask.

(Do YOU have a question about the Rolls-Royce Corniche? Send your query to James May at *Scotland on Sunday*. Remember to mark your envelope 'I bet you've had a lot of free glasses from petrol stations'.)

THE BEST CAR IN THE WORLD – BUT DON'T GET EXCITED

Welcome, readers, to the 100th column I've written for *Telegraph Motoring*. Obviously I've put up some balloons in my office and there will be a collector's limited edition bound in Morocco leather, but in the meantime I thought I should use this momentous occasion to address a very serious topic.

So – what's the best car I've ever driven? As 'that other bloke off *Top Gear*' I'm sometimes approached in pubs and assailed with this very question – usually after a short preamble during which I'm asked where Jezza is (as if I live with him and shouldn't be allowed out on my own) or if I realise that I look a bit like that other bloke off *Top Gear*. And this 'best car' enquiry has always left me a bit stumped up to now.

It would be easy to nominate, say, the Bentley Continental R, one of my favourite cars of all time. But I'm not sure I could universally recommend one. Parking it is an issue, and because it's an aristocrat it has a bit of a drink problem.

I've even driven a Ferrari Enzo, and was surprised how much I liked it. But is it really the best? Not if you're on a budget, wearing a short skirt or wanting to buy some timber from B&Q. Then it's pretty much the worst.

And so it goes on. Best luxury car or best supercar is easy, but what is the unqualified best car I've ever driven? What is the best car I've laid hands on in over a decade of trying out cars, *all things considered*? I spent several hours thinking about this and making lists, and I've finally come up with the answer.

What's more, I've tried the theory out on a group of merchant bankers I was talking to last week. These were intelligent people, with a fearsome grasp of economic theory and global politics. As merchant bankers they all drove Ferraris and Astons and the like. In short, we're not talking here of the sort of car enthusiasts who just shout 'Subaru' regardless of the question.

I suggested to them that the best car I've ever driven, all things considered, was the Citroen AX GT of 1991. Nobody argued, despite being eminently qualified for the job, so I may be on to something.

I admit the AX GT (not, you will note, the later AX GTi, in which Citroen overdid things a bit) is not terribly promising. Constructed from old biscuit tins, powered by a rudimentary 1.4-litre engine and not exactly eye-catching, it would probably kill you in a crash. It was built in France, so was presumably the work of communists.

Then again, if you assume every attribute by which we judge cars is important, it comes out rather well. In 1991 it was cheap at under £9,000 (cars were, you may remember, more expensive then). It reached 60 mph from rest in 9.0 seconds, which is quick enough to be amusing, and could attain 107 mph, which is fast enough to land you in the clanger. Yet on a long run it could easily return over 40 mpg. Wasn't actually ugly, either.

The more I analyse this, the more sense it makes. The AX was short and had small overhangs, so it was wieldy and easy to park. Yet because no one was too worried back then about what happened if you drove into a lamp-post, it was also space efficient and could carry four in reasonable comfort. Entry and egress were easy for the infirm and there was even some space for bags.

It was very light, too, and long before other makers started banging on about weight-saving. Lightness made it fun to drive; it was perky and the responses were immediate, like they are in a really small sports car. Yet this quality was lost on po-faced actuarial types, so it was cheap to insure.

Because it was light, the suspension didn't need to be firm in order to keep the body motion in check. So despite the fine handling the ride was also pretty good. Low weight and low inertia also meant the tyres could be small, which led to that surfeit of 'power' over grip that makes an old Mini so entertaining. Small tyres were also cheaper to replace.

And so it goes on. Pick any other car, and the AX GT will be better than it at something, while remaining plenty good enough at everything else. If Top Trumps could be redesigned to deal with qualitative as well as the purely quantitative attributes of cars, the AX GT would be the card that meant you would win. Since my meeting with the bankers I've tried this theory on a number of colleagues and friends, and no one has yet defeated me in a straight fight.

Try me.

TOO MANY CARS SPOIL LIFE'S MINESTRONE

The following is intended as a cautionary tale for anyone who entertains the ludicrous idea of being a 'car collector'.

There are problems with having more than one. I have four, plus three motorcycles, which is not intended as a boast since they amount to the value of one half-decent new car. It's impossible to arrange tax, MoT and insurance for this little lot such that they all expire at the same time, so barely a day goes by without some tedious motor-related legal document leaping out from a corner of the filing cabinet with a 'so – what you gonna do about it then, eh?' like a tiresome drunk.

But that's only the start. A man called Fred has rung me from Holland. He's the chap who's bought my old Jaguar XJ-6 Coupé, sold to create a garage space for the forthcoming Porsche Boxster, which must surely arrive any day. He's arranged to fly over on Saturday and meet me at home.

Within ten minutes of him texting me to confirm that he'd bought a plane ticket, *Top Gear* TV rang to tell me I was off to the South of France to drive a bothersome Ferrari around. I'd be coming home on – you can probably already guess this – Saturday.

Now – I'm due to arrive at Gatwick an hour after Fred arrives at Stansted. So I warned him, and arranged for someone to be here to entertain him. Fine. Then I realised that the Jaguar lives five miles away, in one of three leased garages, so I thought I'd better get it on the way back from the airport.

Except that the key to the garage door is on the car keys, and these were with my mate Colin, who had been showing the Jag to potential customers in my absence. And he's gone on holiday and won't be back until Saturday.

My mechanic friend Nigel has a spare key for the Jag garage, but of course wouldn't be at work on Saturday. So

I motorcycled over to his workshop on the big Honda, borrowed the garage key, removed the Jag from its garage using my spare car keys, left the bike in the garage, drove back to Nigel's, dropped off the spare garage key, and headed home. I was going to put the Jag in the Porsche 911's garage, which is over the road from my house, and then drive the 911 back to the Jag's garage, put it away and come home again on the bike.

But then I remembered that the 911 had broken down two days ago – something to do with the ignition module. The AA had towed it home for me and I'd pushed it into its garage and locked it up. Clearly, I couldn't push the 911 five miles back to the Jaguar's garage and anyway, I realised, I still didn't have the key for the door. So I hid the Jaguar in the BBC's underground car park, amongst all the diesel hatchbacks and Smart cars. I need to remember to take my BBC car park pass to France.

The 911 is also for sale, and I'd had a charming e-mail from a female reader of *Telegraph Motoring* to say she was coming down from Manchester to see her parents and would like to view the car. On Saturday. But now of course it's broken, and there's no time to mend it because I'm being sent to France.

Somewhere in all this there is also a Bentley T2, but that's of no use because that, also, is in a garage five miles away and the tax has run out. The folding bicycle has a puncture.

And now the cheerful bloke from the Porsche Centre has rung to say that it's good news, Mr May: your new car will be ready for you on – God in heaven – Saturday. That's two days before the insurance on the Range Rover runs out. Do I change the policy to cover the Porsche instead – which means I have to find somewhere to store the Range Rover while I try to sell it – or do I add it, thus committing myself to another year with the faithful old Landy? I have to decide in the half hour left before I go to France so that I can have a cover note issued, otherwise the dealer can't register and tax the new car.

And anyway, the Boxster is supposed to go in the garage where the 911 lives, and the 911 is bust. It can't go in the Jag's garage because it then won't be insured, because it has a different post code. It could go in the garage attached to the house if I move the other bikes out, but of course I can't because the MoT is out on the Guzzi. I now can't remember where I put the big Honda or if I left the Jag's headlights on.

Look – think very hard about the car you want. Then buy that one, brand new. The tax and insurance will be co-terminal, and after three years the MoT will come up at the same time as well.

And then, unlike me, you can do something useful with your life.

THE WAGES OF SIN ARE NOT ENOUGH FOR A NEW PORSCHE

Anyone out there who works regularly on a computer will no doubt have made use of a programme called Stickies. It's a sort of digital version of those annoying little yellow labels used by people in offices, and very handy for keeping your colleagues abreast of things you haven't done yet.

For several months now, I've had a 'Sticky' displayed right across the top of my screen. It reads: 'Remember – you cannot really afford a new Porsche Boxster'. It's been carefully arranged so that whatever I'm doing on the machine, and no matter how many 'applications' are running at once, it admonishes me from the top of the monitor like one of those portentous inscriptions over the gateways of Victorian cemeteries.

However, as I'm a chap, and it is essentially a piece of advice, I've ignored it.

If you're a regular reader you may remember that, a few weeks ago, I ordered the new Boxster S after my local dealer had demonstrated, using Man Maths, that I could afford one. Man Maths, in case you don't know, is a type of Blairite arithmetic designed to show that the customer, who in the Thatcher era we imagined always to be right, is in fact a complete fiscal halfwit.

Having since indulged in some dependable Newtonian calculations, I discover that I have actually saved the colossal sum of £800 towards an impending invoice which, even with the deposit paid, still stands at a rather intimidating £40,019 outstanding. What, exactly, did I imagine I was going to do? £40,019 is not just more money than I've ever spent on anything in my life, it's more money than I've ever even thought of in one go.

Once, in the showroom, the price seemed strangely theoretical, like relativity. It was such a long way off that worrying about it was like worrying about inheritance tax. But now they've phoned to say: great news! The car could be ready by the end of September. I am fast approaching a time when I walk back into the dealership to the accompaniment of that annoying little tune from *Countdown*; the one that tells you the time is up and you've blown it. This, I imagine, is the point at which the salesman stops addressing me as 'Mr May'.

Still, there was always a chance that the perverted science of Man Maths could be defeated, or at least made to balance, with the disposal of what is sometimes known as Man Crap, starting with my pristine 1976 Jaguar XJ 4.2 Coupé.

'Be your own East-End villain,' I proclaimed on eBay, where I advertised the car with a very modest reserve, 'in this totally lock, stock but non-smoking two-door XJ Jaguar!'

Nothing. And in case you're wondering, no one wants the old 911 either; or the N-gauge model railway, or the Weirauch .22 air rifle (with telescopic sight featuring pellet-drop compensation), or the outboard motor, the boat, the Apple Macintosh Classic or the collection of Commando War Stories in Pictures.

I've always argued that cars are actually very good value in relative terms. All that cutting-edge technology, all that manufacturing expertise – it can all be ours, and the greatest triumph of the car is that it makes all this so accessible. Yet I've thrown very little away in life, and everything I've accumulated in adulthood appears to have the worth of an odd sock when weighed in the balance against German sports car engineering. So I was wrong. In absolute terms, cars are still chuffing expensive.

Sorry to talk about money so much this week. I realise, of course, that it's almost as vulgar as owning a very big television. But we are now at the point where I simply cannot afford to beat around the bush any longer. I have ordered, and paid the deposit on, a car to which I am now totally committed, and which I have specified in a colour scheme that no one else will want. And the painful truth is that I have ABSOLUTELY NO MEANS OF PAYING FOR IT. Short of starting a fund and erecting one of those big thermometer-style new-church-roof displays outside my house, I really don't see how I'm going to do it.

Desperate times call for desperate measures, and so, as usual, I reach behind my desk for a book of dead poets. Christopher Marlowe anticipated the problem by several centuries:

Base fortune, now I see,
That in thy wheel there is a point,
To which when men aspire,
They tumble headlong down.

And the Porsche Boxster hadn't even been invented then.

CORNISH SEPARATIST MOUNTS ASSAULT ON CAR UPHOLSTERY

As I think is well known, the Cornish pasty – brilliant though it is in its own right – evolved the way it did for purely practical reasons.

That neat little crimped pastry parcel of meat 'n' two veg was simply a convenient way for Cornish working men, and especially tin miners, to take a meal on the job in the pocket of a donkey jacket, without fear that it would become seriously contaminated by dirt or, worse, spilled. I like to assume that a proper pasty is lightly glazed because that once meant dirt was less likely to stick to it. This was before Tupperware.

I have heard it said by a man who claimed to be some sort of eatymologist (that is, one who studies the historical source of food formats) that the original pasty would have been divided by an interior wall of thin pastry, rather in the way that many Victorian houses are converted into several flats. On one side of the divide would be the savoury filling we're familiar with; on the other, something like stewed apple. That way, you got your main course and a pudding in one convenient pocket-sized package.

So in an earlier era, the Cornish pasty would have been a whole meal in itself. Now, of course, it is but a snack; before long, I imagine, some restaurateur or ridiculous food critic will make the pasty a voguish delicacy, which people will order in poncy restaurants along with a glass of fashionable bitter, and that, as the poet Larkin once observed, will be England gone. In the meantime, though, the pasty is very popular with motorists eating on the move.

And for this reason, I think it needs a bit of a rethink. For while a few flecks of pastry and the odd errant morsel of diced carrot might have gone unnoticed in the dank gloom of the pit, on the dove-pale upholstery of the Bentley they are an absolute disaster. And that is just the thin end of the pasty menace.

What man would not confess that at some time, travelling alone, he has bought a Cornish pasty from a motorway service station? You haven't? Read on.

So you return to the car, start the engine, and pull away onto the slip road. You will probably select second gear before guiltily peeling the wrapper from one end of what once sustained stout men burrowing in the bowels of the earth. And the instant your teeth make contact with the surface of the pasty, the great flaky cataract begins. The yield from even an expertly consumed Cornish pasty is deeply disappointing, and to be honest you may as well open the door of your car and empty the crumb tray from my toaster in there. And that's never been emptied before.

Still – you have another hand, so in an instant you cup that under your chin to catch the fallout. This is not the end, especially if you have been foolhardy enough to heat your pasty in the slimy-doored microwave situated to one side of the filling station's refrigerated pie counter. By now your teeth have met somewhere in the centre of what turns out to be largely a void, but what *is* in there is, of course, red hot. Pasty lava sticks to your face, where, for some reason, it feels even hotter.

You now join the M1 at 70 mph, steering with your knees and, because you are still in second gear, with the engine of your Vauxhall Vectra on the wrong side of 12,000 rpm. I'm not going to be ninnyish enough to suggest that the pasty is a threat to road safety, but at the very least it isn't doing the nation's valve gear a lot of good.

To be honest, this isn't an isolated crisis. Eating on the go is in need of reassessment generally. The cramped economy-class seats of aeroplanes, for example, cry out for a one-utensil, one-implement meal rather than a shrink-wrapped five-course dining experience that you are required to eat off a table smaller than most plates and with less elbow room than I expect in my coffin. The food is already out there: the Orientals give us noodles, the South Americans have chilli, Italy gives us pasta, France a sausage cassoulet and Britain the superior beef stew and dumplings. America has even done away with the need for a fork with the double cheeseburger, and if it gets any bigger they won't need opposed thumbs either.

But in the car, another solution is required. I want someone to apply to the on-road lunch the same intelligence that some unknown heroine in pre-industrial Cornwall applied to her husband's snap box.

Ginsters – you know it's you.

FREE LIGHTBULB WITH EVERY NEW PORSCHE

On two occasions in my life so far I have walked into a motorcycle dealership to buy a new pair of gloves and left with a whole new bike.

These people aren't stupid and lay a fairly simple trap for the unwary rider – the gloves are at the back of the shop, so you have to walk past all the bikes before you get to them. No one ever says, 'Let's put the gloves by the front door so people who only want gloves won't have to pick their way through all the new bikes and those signs advertising easy finance.'

It nearly happened again the other day when, right on cue at two years old and at the time when I might be thinking of replacing the bike, a small hole appeared in one of my biking gloves. So off I went to the nearby Triumph showroom and, half an hour later, was belting through the countryside on a new Speed Triple demonstrator. Immediately after that I went home and did some Man Maths, which is a type of creative accountancy designed to show that a new bike isn't really going to cost anything at all.

I'm sure we've all been here – motorcycle dealerships, boat yards, those shops that sell sit-on lawn mowers – and I started wondering: did the desire for a new Speed Triple mug me unexpectedly as I entered the bike showroom, or was I subconsciously using the lightly damaged item of protective clothing to legitimise a test ride? Am I a victim of salesmanship, or my own worst enemy?

Well, now I know it's the former, because a few days ago I went into a car dealership in all innocence looking to buy a new light bulb and am now perilously close to buying a new car.

The only thing that has ever gone wrong with my old 911 is a blown indicator bulb. And when I went to my local Porsche dealer to buy a new one, the man behind the spares counter simply gave it to me rather than subject me to the convoluted stream of paperwork that, for some reason, always accompanies the sale of small car spares. Thus he earned an immediate and shameless plug in this column for AFN Porsche of Chiswick, purveyors of free bulbs to the discerning Porsche enthusiast. Or at least anyone who goes in waving this newspaper and saying, 'You didn't charge this bloke'.

But the warm glow of 'customer' satisfaction was simply a technique to blind me to the oldest trick in the book – namely, positioning the door to the spares department diagonally opposite the main entrance to the showroom. That meant I had to walk through conditioned air thick with the whiff of Porsche leather, past glittering brochures, a beaming lady attending the TCMF[4] and, of course, the serried ranks of new and nearly-new Porsches. I have to say that my nearby Land Rover outlet gets this all wrong. Their spares department is reached through a small door on the side of the building, which explains why, despite having had to replace several bulbs and a few fuses on the old Range Rover over the last two years, I'm still not driving a new Defender.

Anyway. Amongst all the cars in the Porsche emporium was the new Boxster S. I really like the new Boxster. In fact, we'd been talking about it on the programme the day before, since Hammond and Clarkson have got it into their witless heads that the Mercedes SLK is somehow a better car. I paused only for a second or two next to a blue one but in that time a bright chap with good teeth approached. He kept calling me 'Mr May', which made me feel like a bank manager and the sort of bloke who could actually afford a Porsche Boxster. He even had a hand-held computer that did Man Maths and proved that, actually, I

---

[4] Tea and coffee making facilities.

could. Then I took one for a test-drive and that, frankly, was a mistake.

Where does this end? Well, it hasn't yet. Every day I receive a polite text message with details of new payment plans and options prices. I thought I could fend them off by telling them I wanted green seats but a black dashboard with red instruments. But a few hours later another message arrived to say that they'd spoken directly to the factory and, yes, they could do that. Bugger. It seems there is no escape.

Free bulb my arse. If the indicator goes on your old 911, do yourself a favour and buy a replacement from Halfords. The worst that can happen is that you'll come away with a new socket set.

NO OPTIONS IS THE ONLY OPTION

Hello readers. I must warn you that I'm going to be rather boring this month, so if you've got any ironing to do I suggest you get on with it while you're waiting for the next column to start.

The thing is that for the very first time in my life I've bought a brand new car, and unfortunately it's made me jolly cross. With Ferrari.

And no, I haven't bought a Ferrari. But this all began when Jeremy started investigating the options list on the new F430, and discovered a few examples of the unexplained. If you want red brake calipers, that's an extra £500. Maybe that's fair enough. Maybe special heat-resistant red paint is expensive and difficult to apply. But if you want yellow calipers, that'll be £560.

Why is this? As far as I can see, painting the calipers yellow instead of red involves nothing more than the caliper-painting man reaching for a tin of yellow instead of a tin of red. So where does the extra £60 come from, eh? I suppose if you're spending around £120,000 on a car the odd £60 is neither here nor there; then again, if you're charging £120,000 for a car it's neither here nor there either, so that's no excuse.

And then there's the seat stitching. One way or another, the seats have to be sewn together, otherwise you'd soon end up with a pile of useless leather in the footwell. But if you select a special colour for the thread, it costs you £260. Now – as far as I can make out, this involves nothing more than the seat-stitcher inserting a different reel of cotton into the sewing machine, and that operation simply cannot be worth £260 even at Ferrari. Just to be certain of my ground here, I've been to John Lewis and can confirm that £260 would buy enough thread to sew Guy Fawkes and all of his chums back together.

When I thought about it, I realised this sort of thing has been going on for years. I remember a time when BMW charged extra for something called, I think, the 'smoker delete package'. This involved removing the ashtray and lighter and blanking off the resulting holes, which is a bit churlish really since those bits they took out could then be used on another car. So not only were they relieving you of the money you'd saved by not buying any fags, they were also saving themselves a few bob into the bargain. That was a doppel whammy for Bavarian book-keeping.

And so it goes on. To get to the point: I've now ordered a new Porsche Boxster S, because Porsche are upfront and their option pricing is transparent. The Boxster is the best mid-priced roadster and my faith in it can only increase following the revelation that those halfwits Hammond and Clarkson think the Mercedes SLK is somehow a better car.

I know what you're thinking; you're thinking, *bet he did a deal with Porsche because he works for* Top Gear *and they gave him a big discount,* but you'd be as wrong as the big gay one and the irritating little sod are about German sports cars. I went into my local dealership like anyone else and ordered it at the full price.

(The honest truth is that I went into my local Porsche shop to buy a replacement light bulb for my old 911, but was seduced by the charming lady with the tea and biscuits, the brochures and every other device used by the salesman to part the fool from the money he doesn't even have. But anyway.)

This is where the whole thing becomes . . . I was about to say interesting, but then I remembered that I've already admitted how boring it is. Bear with me.

The completely standard Boxster S is something that only really exists in theory, a bit like hyperspace. What we think of as 'the Boxster S' should really be considered in the way that Spain is; ie not finished yet. This is because it's designed to be 'personalised'.

So I ordered the full leather interior, which cost me £1,150. Then I ordered a special, non-standard leather colour, cocoa brown, which added another £1,395. But I said I wanted the steering wheel in black. That's what I would have got if I'd just ordered the standard black interior, and it wouldn't have cost me anything. Fair?

I never said this was going to be gripping and, to be frank, it gets worse.

Now Porsche say they want another £500 for the black steering wheel. How can this be? It's the steering wheel they would have been obliged to put on if I hadn't said anything, if you see what I mean. Unless they're going to admit to the folly of producing a brown steering wheel and then re-trimming it in the black it would have been in the first place, I should really be given a small discount for saving a bit of brown leather.

I have to say that the dealership has been perfectly charming about all this and its staff are clearly as embarrassed as I am perplexed. So eventually I rang Porsche themselves. They told me it was something to do with an XP90 ordering code, or some such blarney, which is completely meaningless to the man, like me, on the street. They say if I don't want the brown steering wheel I have to pay for an optional sports steering wheel. In black. But I don't want a sports steering wheel; I want the unused one gathering dust in the parts bin. They're asking me to pay to remove an option I've already paid to have in the first place, which is a bit like ordering a pizza margarita with extra anchovies and then slipping the waiter a couple of quid to get rid of the anchovies and just put some more cheese on instead.

The whole thing is so boring I'm beginning to bore myself, but at least I've finally come up with a case for the Nissan Murano. This is a very good car but one I don't particularly like – it's too brash, and its teeth are too chromed. What I do like, however, is that there are no options to be had on it. Everything is standard, and anything that isn't standard can't be had at all.

You either buy it, or you don't buy it. In fact, it's the best car on sale in Britain today.

THE GREAT TRANSPORT DEBATE

MOTORWAY SERVICES – IS THIS AN OXYMORON OR WHAT?

At the risk of sounding like some patronising white liberal, I really enjoy the multi-cultural England. But I want it to be just that – several cultures living side by side in some sort of harmony. I don't want our differences brushed aside or subsumed under euphemisms as if they're something distasteful, in the way we discuss bowel disorders; I'm still a pompous old fart who talks about the war and laughs at the Germans and I still want to find my favourite tandoori staffed by real Indians who no longer give me the menu but ask me straight off vhat I am vanting. Differences are something to be enjoyed.

Having now established myself as some sort of bigot in the minds of those who prefer beards, bicycles and cable-knit, I must add that amongst all this I still want to find the real England. I'm no misty-eyed nostalgist either, and I firmly believe that the good old days were largely awful, but there are bits of Blighty worthy of preservation at all cost. I'm not talking about the pomp of royal occasion or the affected tweeness of cricket on the village green, I'm referring to more ordinary phenomena like the seaside prom and the (un-themed) local pub. And leading the roll-call of institutions that made the nation great is my local café.

Here is an establishment in the true sense, in the sense we wrongly apply to parliament or the church. It is run by a dignified, even glamorous, middle-aged woman, while in the dim background, towering over grill, hotplate and pan, is an awesome figure of a man who serves up the tastiest dishes that ever were tasted. What Trusthouse Forte would probably call the breakfast experience is variable, but it varies between the merely good and the religious. Have that tea on me, sir. Well, thanks very much. As long as this and thousands of caffs like it survive, Shakespeare can rest in peace with the epithet 'this other Eden'.

However, this ideal goes to pot as soon as you hit the road. I've never been able to explain it, but every service attendant specifically on the motorist is tainted with tackiness. Garages are still largely distrusted, petrol station shops offend with old tat and voucher schemes, quick-fit repair centres leave you feeling as grubby as an old exhaust baffle. Leading the field in motoring-related misery, though – *still* – is the motorway service station.

I've been avoiding these places for years, preferring instead the Little Chef – far and away the best shot yet at putting a franchise face on the local caff principle. But today Little Chef was full and waiting, so I moved on to the corporate colossus down the road. Even as I joined the queue with my slimy tray I knew this was a mistake. There on the counter were 'breakfast items' made bland by company strategy and being kept warm. A lethargic woman piled my order haphazardly on the plate and left it standing while she went to fetch my egg – cooked one at a time while the queue of fellow Little Chef disappointeds amassed behind me – and then broken in transit.

No worry, though, surely faith would be restored at the most important part of the process, the tea counter. I said, 'A pot of tea, please' and expected to be assailed with something like 'coming right up, Sir' or 'Ceylon or India, Sir?' But no, he gestured dismissively at the counter: 'Zwun there ready.' How long had it been there? One minute? Twenty? And the knob had come off the lid. Anger flared up like a neglected deep-fat fryer; I wanted to seize this snivelling cretin by the throat and yell *Do you know what you're doing, you fool, you're running the country down*, but he'd already walked off. The girl at the till spoke only enough to announce the ludicrous price before I shuffled off to my seat.

It was tepid at best, the bacon looked flaccid and the beans were translucent: good God, I wouldn't be surprised to learn that they'd been *microwaved*. As I ate I could hear the marketing people talk grandly of variety and the total customer experience. Yes, the counters were stuffed with irrelevancies like croissants, Danish pastries, muesli, mineral water and even a cringeworthy and misplaced attempt to muscle in on the curry culture; everything was 'your choice of', 'for you' and there was a sign in the bogs outlining my right to complain if the 'facilities' disappointed in any way. Yet the place was a monument to mediocrity run by mutants, being gradually turned, like England's airports and railway stations, into a glorified shopping centre and at the expense of my beloved breakfast. My local café, with its swiftly delivered God's-own bubble and squeak, could wipe the floor with this lot, and it's they who should be running it.

Churchill said that he wanted to revive the grand old name of England. Me too, and as with any daunting task it begins with a good fry-up. Now, could someone please do me a bacon sandwich, I'm bloody starving.

THE TRAIN NOW DEPARTING FROM MY BEDROOM

I've decided that this column, though essentially a motoring forum, should be open to other modes of transport. Cars, after all, may not always be with us, so we need to be prepared. This month I'd like to consider railways.

In fact I'd like to settle once and for all this question of the viability of rail transport, using what town planners and civil engineers call a 'model'. I have been studying railways in microcosm, and I have to say the signs are not good.

This experiment began with an old chum in the pub, where we debated trains and whether or not there was a place for them in the modern transport scheme of things. Then we retired to the house, where the best Scotch dwindled rapidly but still no agreement could be reached. In the end there was only one thing for it – get the train set out.

Now if I were twelve, I'd be boasting confidently that my train set is better than yours. Not for the May household a humble oval of track around which the *Flying Scotsman* circulates endlessly with realistic chuffing sound. Oh no. This thing, amassed by me through childhood and early teenage, lives in a towering pile of boxes and has been lugged around with me from home to home throughout all my adult life. I've often looked at it but never put it all together, and when I opened the giant box containing all the track I remembered why.

Anyone who has had a train set of any complexity will know that the trick is to concoct a layout using every last piece of track. If you push it all together and find one piece of R603 second-radius half-curve left over, there's only one thing to do and that's pull it all to bits and start again. As my set includes over 35 pairs of points and the operating turntable, this took some time. It certainly saw the last of the Scotch off.

There is a host of goods rolling stock and coaches and some 25 locomotives, several of which are from the 50s and came down to me through some tangential arm of the family, so are probably quite collectable. Or were, before matey boy trod on them. Opening the doors on the twin-bogie container carrier, I discovered some liquorice torpedoes c.1970.

With the whole thing up and running many hours later, a few examples of rank inauthenticity revealed themselves. Mallard may hold the world steam speed record at 126 mph (don't worry, I had to look that up) but the 00-gauge version can manage at least ten times that with terrifying consequences through tight bends. Also, if you or I threw ourselves under a train we would be completely annihilated, but when the headless stationmaster falls from his platform onto the up main line, he can derail the entire five-coach *Flying Scotsman*, cutting its evocative high-speed progress stone dead in mid-realistic-chuff, and emerge unscathed. I'd also like to think that real train drivers are in a slightly more alert state than we were.

On the other hand, certain problems encountered in running the train set sound painfully familiar. For one thing, all the signals were wrong, which at one point caused a 4-6-0 Fowler tender locomotive to be diverted, regulator fully open, straight down a siding and into a cardboard engine shed at 1,000 mph. Fortunately it was only hauling a coal train. There aren't actually that many coaches in the set because I was never disciplined enough to save up for them. A coach cost around four times as much as a coal truck, so as soon as I'd saved up a quarter of its price I'd give in and just buy the truck.

Points failure – there's another thing. The prompt arrival of the 03.30 express from the bedroom to the sitting room depends entirely on the shape and cleanliness of a minute copper contact on what is known as the 'blade' (looked that up too) of the points. The existence of these things has generated, over the years, a steady migration of emery boards from sister's bedroom to train box.

The engines break down as well. We all know about the problem of leaves on the line; in 00-scale, it is the scenic medium known as fluff, modelled in the very popular scale of twelve inches to the foot. In real life, the equivalent would be a man-sized ball of tumbleweed blowing under the power unit of your local suburban train and cacking up the commutator, requiring Railtrack to unscrew the plastic bodywork and extract it with a gigantic pair of tweezers, losing the screw in the process.

But the real failing of the railway was poignantly demonstrated by an attempt to deliver a five-plank wagon load of Bombay Mix to my mate slumped in the corner. The railway didn't go there. It went under sofas and beds, around the TV and through tunnels and cuttings cunningly wrought from cushions and beer tins. But not where the perishable goods were actually needed, which was in the karzi. And I was buggered if I was going to redesign it again.

And there's the problem. It's all very well saying that freight should be put back on the railways, but there's no branch line running to my local Sainsbury's, which is where we buy our buns. So the final leg of the journey, through town, is always going to be by truck.

So that's that then. The train set is back in its boxes and I can confidently predict that the railways are doomed. Now where are my old Dinkies?

THIS PRECIOUS CAR, SET IN A SILVER SEA

I never expected to like the Vauxhall Monaro VXR quite so much as I do. It's not as if it's a real Vauxhall: it's actually an Australian Holden, which is shipped into Luton and given to a bloke who prises off the Holden badge and replaces it with a Vauxhall one. Since he only has one simple typesetting job to do, he might have made an effort to do it in the same font, but no. Imagine if my name was set at the top of this column as James May and you'll get an idea of just how unconvincing this car looks from the back.

There are other reasons why I shouldn't like it. The styling is locked somewhere in the late 80s, it's not exactly presented as a gentleman's express, and Holden designed the interior by taking a diagram of the MkIII Cavalier's cabin and enlarging it on a photocopier. First thing in the morning, when the gearbox oil is still cold, you need a neighbour to help you put it into reverse. And now I've discovered that Jeremy Clarkson likes it, which would normally put an automatic bar on its acceptability.

But, so help me, the man who admits to driving 'as though my trousers are on fire' seems to have a point. This 5.7-litre V8 rear-drive muscle car is about as sophisticated and unsurprising as a stag party in Sydney, but is all the better for it. It has about it the flavour of a 90s Aston Martin Vantage, and I really can't be kinder than that about it.

I was enjoying the Monaro so much that I began to think it would be a good idea to drive to the coast, hop on a ferry, and take the Fauxhall over to the continent, where its performance potential could be more fully exploited, since I would be abroad. But then, by one of those amazing coincidences that attends the column-writer's craft, a terrible piece of news came over the big-buttoned Australian-spec radio.

P&O Ferries, it seems, is about to shed 1200 of its staff as part of a rationalisation process in response to growing competition from the channel tunnel and the no-frills airlines. And I can see why. The Chunnel is quicker and ultimately easier, and the last European flight I took on easyJet was so ludicrously cheap that I think I spent more money on a sandwich from the in-flight Easy Trolley. The ferry is definitely under threat.

But whenever possible, I still prefer to take it. For one thing, the ferry has improved a lot in the last few years, probably in response to increased competition from the Channel Tunnel and the no-frills airlines. The galley is much better, the service is more punctual and the bearded bloke on the bridge is definitely putting his foot down, or whatever it is you do on a boat.

Of course, comes the retort from the ferry's detractors, you will never be seasick in the tunnel. They're right. I have been on a crossing so rough that on entering the gentleman's 'head' I was confronted by a man lying in a pool of his own vomit who begged me to kill him.

So I can only conclude that he was a foreigner. The spiritual descendants of Drake, Cook and the Pilgrim Fathers would have absolutely no idea of his suffering. Seasickness is for Belgian caravaners, not the British.

More important than any of this is the inescapable fact that the ferry is the only link to the continent that instils in its passengers the appropriately foreboding sense that one is leaving the sceptred isle behind. Little compares to the wrench of separation felt on seeing the White Cliffs receding into the watery mist, but by dint of this the unalloyed joy of homecoming is raised to the height of pure ecstasy.

I feel that, as British motorists, we have a moral and historical duty to patronise the ferry. It's more fun, it imparts more of a sense of adventure, and it allows us, on our return, to experience what Hitler, Napoleon and the

King of Spain could never achieve with all their pomp and big talk – namely, a seaborne landing in the Other Eden.

And remember – those same white cliffs, re-emerging from the gloom that lesser peoples might imagine would leave the continent cut off, will help to remind you why you took a European holiday in the first place.

Which was to remind yourself how lucky you are to live in Britain.

A RIGHT MERRY DING-DONG WITH TWO CAR MAGAZINES

Christmas is coming and there are several things I don't like about it. Commercialism, comedy Christmas cards, Porsche 911 soap-on-a-rope, overdone sprouts, cuff links, women with tinsel in their hair, self-styled orators who say 'Marley was dead' in a too-dramatic voice, apologists who say 'Well, of course, it was originally a pagan festival' in a too-smug voice, the alternative Queen's Speech, the hard ones in Quality Street and my neighbourhood's atonal carol singers.

But my least favourite bit is that moment, usually late on Christmas day afternoon, when somebody says, 'Let's play a game'.

In my house, the games live in a dark and largely unexplored cupboard in a corner of the sitting room. And they're all rubbish. Trivial Pursuit? It's awful. People won't admit to not knowing something and the whole process is fraught with argument, including the one over whether the playing counters are called 'pieces of pie' or 'pieces of cheese'. Monopoly? Most of my friends spend far too long talking about the value of their property as it is. Pictionary is pointless and charades is just downright embarrassing.

The problem with games is that, beyond the iconic Top Trumps, there are none about cars. The nearest thing is that seminal card in Escape From Colditz that allows you to steal the German staff car. Unfortunately, however, there is no one left in the world who will agree to be the Germans, so the game never starts anyway. Even my German friends won't be the Germans any more.

This year, though, things are looking up, because my colleague Richard Hammond and I have invented a new game. It's called Fantasy Crap Car Garage and here are the rules.

You will need:

Two compatible magazines with motoring small ads: say, *Auto Trader* and *Exchange & Mart*, or *Classic Cars* and *Classic and Sports Car*
Two A4 sheets of cardboard
A Pritt Stick
Scissors
Two pencils
A stopwatch
The Macallan, or a similar single malt

The object of the game is to assemble an imaginary garage of ten rubbish cars on your sheet of A4 cardboard.

A toss of a coin decides on who begins the game, and the winning player calls the criteria for the first round, which must include a maximum price and two other attributes. Examples might be 'French, two-door, up to £5,000' or '1990s, V6, up to £500.' Which, let's face it, is a Granada Scorpio.

The watch is started and the two players scour the small ads for suitable vehicles. When a player has found one he calls 'garage', after which the remaining player has thirty seconds left in which to find a car. Once the watch has been stopped the players compare ads and decide who has 'bought' the most interesting and desirable car.

Admittedly, the rules do not offer a definitive guide to who has won here, which is why the single malt is included in the games equipment. But it does stimulate interesting debate and one instinctively knows when the other bloke is right. In the event of a draw, since many small ads are duplicated between magazines, the round is null and void.

The winner cuts out his car and glues it to his cardboard 'garage', with the Pritt Stick. The loser cuts his out and puts it in the bin. This has a far-reaching impact on the progress of the game, since any car on the other side of the page is also lost. It is not worth playing a shabby MkIII Escort if there's a cheap Jag overleaf that might be needed later.

If the winner's car comes in under budget, then the excess is noted in a corner of the garage, using the pencil. This additional budget can be used by the winner in whole or part *for the next round only*.

The magazines are swapped, the loser calls the new criteria, and the whole gay, mad whirl starts all over again.

As an added refinement, a 'trump colour' made be called, which means that any car meeting the criteria and in the trump colour automatically wins. So, for example, in 'British, four-door, up to £10,000, trumps are beige' a £300 beige Allegro beats a £9,500 green Bentley and gives the winner £9,700 to spend in the next round.

Sorry if this has read a bit like the rules for Risk, but trust me – we've tried it, and it works. It's good, clean, cheap, non-family entertainment. After several hours you will have a fascinating collection of Crap Car Garages, which you can peruse for pleasure on Boxing Day.

But only until eight o'clock, because then *Top Gear*'s on.

WE ALL LIVE IN A WORLD OF YELLOW MARGARINE

One day, when I've had enough of all this, I'm going to sell up and open an unfashionable London West End restaurant with a few like-minded chums.

The food in this place is going to be terrific. All the ingredients will be top-notch, gloriously un-mucked-about-with and painfully fresh. Seasonal vegetables will spring from the bosom of the earth and arrive at the pit of the stomach having lingered only to be rinsed of dirt and lightly steamed or roasted. Anyone who orders the trout will be given a CD of the Schubert quintet of the same name to listen to, because that's how long it will take for the fish to make its way from the waters of the Itchin to your table, courtesy of my angling motorcycle courier. The birds of the forest will still be open-mouthed as the berries snatched from under their beaks dissolve on your tongue.

It isn't even going to be expensive, and for two crucial reasons. Unlike The Ivy, where Posh 'n' Becks hang out, footballers, television personalities, racing drivers, 'it' girls and fashion designers will be barred. And (also unlike the Ivy, I imagine) everything on the menu will be served in the form of a pie.

I've become rather bored of pretentiousness in food, and my restaurant will be the antidote to it. And, God knows, it's long overdue, because even motorway service stations are now preparing meals arranged vertically and idiotically described as, for example, 'oven roast'.

In the meantime, there's the new Michelin guide to eating out in pubs, and as a committed A and B roader, this is the sort of book I need in the glovebox. It's arranged by region, which makes sense, and as Michelin also make maps, it tells you with some authority exactly where each pub is. Not only does it describe the food, it also treats real beer with the dignity it deserves. It even tells you which pubs offer accommodation, in case the lure of Lancaster Bomber becomes too much.

But it's still not perfect. I'm familiar with quite a few of the pubs in the guide, and can vouch for the Michelin man's good taste. But then I tried an unknown one and, horrors, it turned out to be (and in fairness the book does warn you) a gastropub.

It was rubbish. The staff were poncy and pretended to be European, even though one of them was obviously from Bristol, and the food was overpriced and over-prepared. They must have been suffering from some sort of crockery shortage, because mine came in a cereal bowl.

I decided there and then to form a new culinary movement called AGA – the Anti-Gastropub Association. And the first thing we need to do is to commission Michelin to produce yet another glovebox gazetteer; the Michelin guide to eating out in the laybys of Britain.

I've always had a sneaking fondness for those no-star caravan-based establishments. Cresting a rise somewhere in Gloucestershire recently, I saw, in the valley below, the greasy grey smudge that could only be the roof of a burger van. That meant it was all downhill to a chipped cup of navvy's and a bacon bun. Brilliant. I couldn't have been happier if Anthony Worrall-Thompson was at the roadside flagging me down with a frying pan.

There is an inevitability to the Moto services and even the village pub, but a burger van can sometimes heave into view with such suddenness that there are but a few seconds in which to decide whether to go for red or brown sauce. The most permanent are afforded old breeze blocks under each corner and some blow-away plastic picnic furniture; but some are more fleeting. One I have known has no name, and is advertised only with a roughly hewn piece of cardboard propped against a fence and bearing the single word 'open', writ large in wax crayon. It's always open.

This, surely, is what the caravan was invented for; for allowing itinerant chefs to circumvent the finer points of health and safety and, for that matter, customs and excise. Motorcyclists will know the joy of rolling up at Bob's Diner after an hour of toiling at the controls of the metal beast, secure in the knowledge that nothing is going to be pan-fried or served on a bed of ... Or even on a plate. So that'll be a pie then, served by a reassuringly fat bloke.

Sooner or later, these places will be outlawed by some fatuous European legislation because they have no lavatories, or some such nonsense. In the meantime, we need them, because these days even a pub cannot absolutely be relied upon to serve you an honest nosebag. Until my restaurant is open, these vans are all we have.

The proposed name of my restaurant, by the way: The Pievy.

AND YOU THOUGHT OTHER CAR MAGAZINES WERE BORING

There I was, beginning to think that the motoring magazine market was becoming far too anal. The other week I found myself reading a whole and learned journal on the weighty topic of the Golf GTi. Nothing else, just the Golf GTi.

What could be more boring than that? Well, it arrived on my desk this morning, in a plain brown envelope, and sent by the motoring editor of the *Sunday Express* regional newspaper; a man who boasted that he had access to 'the most tedious motoring-related publication in the world'. And he was right.

Now I have read quite a few car-makers' turgid corporate magazines in my time and I'm ashamed to say I've contributed to one or two. I have scanned the AA magazine over my breakfast and I have read Johnny Clarkson's *Sunday Times* column. I once even read the *Guild of Motoring Writers'* newsletter. But nothing, *nothing*, could have prepared me for the June issue of *Parking News*.

Parking News is the mouthpiece of the British Parking Association and is probably not normally available to the public. There's no price or bar-code displayed, so presumably you have to pay at a machine situated half a mile away. How much it actually costs must depend on how long you want to spend reading it.

Not long. How boring is *Parking News*? It's very boring. There's a picture of a car park on the cover. Every feature begins with a gigantic mugshot of its author, who is the same bloke in the same suit with a variety of stick-on haircuts, although one feature kicks off with a photograph of a parking meter. There are more blurred pictures of men shaking hands at conferences and yet more of cars parking. Here is an extract from the news:

New car park opens in Bournemouth.

Possibly of more interest is the feature 'Rage against traffic wardens and parking attendants', which I take to be an edict to the community at large, and 'Study shows millions of victims of car park crime', which I assume would strike a chord with anyone who's ever had to use one. Other excess penalty reading material includes 'The internet and parking', 'Cost 342 – parking policies and their effect on mobility and the local community', and 'Car park fraud – an abridged history'.

I can't really offer a comprehensive digest of its contents in such a short space, but if I pick a series of pertinent phrases from its exhausting range of features I think you'll get the drift: wide variety of growth; trade mission; Norwich City Council; customer service improvements; boost to transport; machine malfunctions; low on tickets; series of seminars; value-added proximity services; I became involved in the parking industry in 1974.

To be fair, though, the creators of *Parking News* have entered the ruthless car park of automotive publishing with no 20p pieces in their ashtrays. It's hardly a subject to warm the cockles of the lonely pay-booth attendant's heart of a cold Friday night. Parking is not really motoring, it's what you have to do when you're not motoring. Parking is to driving what a speed hump is to Silverstone.

So the British Parking Association should be commended on being able to sustain a magazine at all. Parking may seem like a terrifyingly narrow topic for a journal, but the breadth of the organisation's expertise is remarkable. By way of illustration, and in the style of *Have I Got News For You*, I have reproduced here without permission some excerpts from the June issue with the key words removed. Can you guess what they are?

(1) This new _____ _____ is perfectly situated to facilitate access to Bournemouth's main pedestrianised shopping centre.

(2) The _____ _____ has been transformed.

(3) Staff who work at _____ _____ may perhaps receive relatively low rates of pay.

(4) Glaxo-Wellcome and Honda UK, along with several public _____ _____, already use the automatic number-plate reading system.

(5) John Foster has worked in the _____ industry since 1974.

(6) Motorists, upon entering a _____ _____, would be given a time/dated ticket which had upon it a unique, non-sequential four-digit number.

(7) _____ _____ in one form or another have been around as long as the car itself.

(8) Flexcrete launches _____ _____ decking system.

(9) After the scene she entered the _____ _____ and passed her ticket on to her husband.

(10) The transport bill is _____ but highly important.

Incidentally, *Parking News* is 'the No 1 journal for parking professionals'. Does anyone out there have a copy of the other one?

ANSWERS

(1) car park (2) car park (3) car parks (4) car parks (5) parking (6) car park (7) car parks (8) car park (9) car park (10) boring

YOUR MOTHER SHOULD KNOW, BUT ON THIS OCCASION DOESN'T

I believe there is a part of every man that secretly wants a motorcycle. I also think I understand why.

The motorcycle is the nearest thing we have to the charger of the medieval knight of myth and legend. The biker buckles on his armour (and early armour was leather, as it had been for the Romans), mounts his faithful steed and goes to the fight of good, searching, alone, through the intellectual vacuum, in pursuit of an inner truth. Or maybe a chip shop. Personally, I tend to end up like Sir Kay in *Morte D'Arthur*, 'wandering through the wilderness, his wits quite gone from him'. But no matter: where the car driver is merely a commuter, the motorcyclist – even when he is only on the way to the office – is a road warrior.

Consider this: in America and Britain there are religious motorcycle clubs called things like Riders for God and Christ on a Bike, people who quest through the spiritual wasteland to spread the good word. I've never heard of anyone doing this from the driving seat of an Italian supercar.

There are more prosaic reasons for enjoying a motorbike. In a car, you are a passive recipient of the forces that make up Newton's laws of motion; on a bike, you have an active part to play in reacting to every action even when stationary, since if you don't support the bike, it will fall over, and for the same reason that the apple landed on the bewigged physicist's head.

Once, when out on my bike, I put my boot on a discarded piece of chewing gum at some traffic lights. Believe it or not, this actually affected the handling, since it hampered the minute movements of my foot upon the peg. That's how intimately a motorcycle rider is embroiled in the dynamics of the machine, and it's this purity that makes the experience strangely thrilling.

Yes, we have to wear German beer-drinking trousers and they're not wholly acceptable in some restaurants. But even so, motorcycling is honest, uncomplicated and harmless. Unless you fall off. And that brings me neatly to Jeremy's case for the Ariel Atom.

You'll have seen this on the Boxing Day edition of *Top Gear*, assuming your telly didn't break down the day before. If it did, well, the Atom, said Jez, is what middle-aged men heading for a mid-life crisis should buy instead of the motorcycle they want because they weren't allowed one when they were young. It's a sort of minimalist supercar with no real bodywork and not much else either. As a 41-year-old heading for a mid-life crisis and riding a big motorbike because my mum wouldn't let me have one when I was young, I was curious. It's much safer and more exciting than a bike, said the big bloke with the curious aversion to leatherwear, and in any case, it would be faster in a race round the track than a CBR 600RR.

My first objection to this suggestion was that the Atom is a highly specialised machine, while the Honda is only a mid-ranking motorcycle straight out of the crate. This would be a bit like pitching a supercar against the 1916 De Havilland DH2 pusher biplane and then claiming that cars are faster than aeroplanes.

My other objection to the case for the Atom is that it's not actually a car. If your car had come with no roof, no doors, no carpet, no seat adjustment, no cup holder, no radio, no boot, no upholstery and no windscreen, you'd want your money back. As it is, this 'car' – what would probably be called an 'unfinished project' in the pages of *Car and Car Conversions* – is the best part of £40,000.

It actually seems to owe more to bike design anyway. As with a bike, all the mechanical bits are gloriously on show and thus in need of regular and tiresome cleaning. The scaffolding on which it is all mounted owes an obvious debt to the trellis frame of the Ducati Monster. The engine is a modified Honda V-Tec Civic unit, one of the finest four-pot motors in the world and one whose high-rev histrionics can undoubtedly be traced in no small part to Honda's motorcycle racing heritage. You are not required by law to wear a helmet in the Atom, but if Jeremy's face was anything to go by, it's probably a good idea.

And finally, the Atom is not really usable as a normal car would be. There's no roof, so the rain comes in. But I'm on dodgy ground here, since the philosophy runs that the Atom is a second car, a toy, just to be taken out on nice days for pure fun. And I have to admit, if I'm absolutely honest, that's exactly how I use the bike. If it's pissing down or January I take the car. Sallying forth in search of the meaning of existence can be buggered. It's only a hobby, not a way of life.

And so to the 'car' vs bike race. I'm afraid he was right. The Atom posted the second-fastest time around our test track after the Ferrari Enzo's, and even then it was only half a second off. And it beat the Honda by about four seconds.

And what you won't have seen is that it beat a Fireblade as well. In fact I'm fairly convinced that no bike could match the Atom around our twisty track, since a good time, as we have proved over and over again with cars like the Lotus Exige, is about cornering speed rather than outright performance. Bikes look impressive in corners but they're not actually that good at them, and going beyond the limits means you have to complete the lap in the back of an ambulance.

So, to summarise: the Atom is faster than a bike. It's certainly safer than a bike. You don't have to wear a helmet or an ox's former buttocks to drive it, it won't fall over if you forget to put the stand down, and although it's pretty pricey by bike standards it is, according to its V5 document, a car, and the only car faster costs around twelve times as much.

I can see only one problem. Take a look at it. Imagine yourself driving it down a winding country road. How are you going to look to someone coming the other way?

Like someone whose mum still won't let him have a motorbike.

THE DULL RED GLOW OF TECHNOLOGY

WHERE WE WILL BE DRIVING WHEN I'M DEAD

This month, I was going to pen an incisive and thought-provoking piece about the curious smell of the screen-wash in my mate's new BMW 3-series. But hell, I'm not here to provoke deep thought, I'm just here to keep you amused for a couple of minutes. So I've decided to stick with a straightforward knockabout subject: the future of transport.

But in case you're expecting a tiresome rant about integrated strategy, or whatever it is the lefties are always going on about, let me reassure you that I'm talking here about the distant future of transport; a future so remote that we can think only in terms of broad concepts rather than nut 'n' bolt practicalities. I find this sort of thing very exciting. In fact, these thoughts have just dragged me out of the puborama, and that normally requires something really momentous, like a kebab.

Weird – I headed for the pub intending to do the crossword in the *Daily Telegraph*, but I left with a lucid vision of what will happen long after I've qualified for my harp. Beer, as usual, is the answer.

Anyway – let's begin by sorting out what the long-term future of transport isn't. Firstly, it isn't public. Public activities have been in decline for generations. We used to have public baths, but now everyone has one in the house. I used to go to the public library, but now I go to Amazon.com. Even the public house is under threat as more and more people turn to fruit-based drinks from France and consume them at home.

If a finance company can ring and offer me a credit card 'tailored to my individual needs' there is no reason why I should tolerate a mode of transport that sets off from somewhere other than where I live and arrives at some-where other than exactly where I want to go, especially if it requires me to snuggle up to a bloke with ox-felling halitosis. No, the future of transport is personal.

Which so far has meant a car propelled by internal combustion, something that clearly needs improving. And despite what some people might try and tell me, the electric car is not nearly a big enough leap forward for my liking. Electricity is notoriously difficult to store, tricky to generate cleanly in any quantity, and a remarkably inefficient way of transferring energy. And even if all these problems were overcome, electric cars would still make a really irritating noise.

Not bio-fuel either. This is fine if you live in Brazil, where there aren't that many cars and millions of spare acres in which to grow rape seed. But farmland is too precious in places like Europe and the Far East. It's needed for golf courses. And we should forget any notion of growing bio fuel crops at home in Dig for Victory style – space is at such a premium where I live in West London that it's as much as I can do to grow a small bay tree at either side of my front step, and I only do that so I can say, 'Oh no, the bay leafs are at the door'.

So that takes us to the fuel-cell car, which so far looks quite promising. Providing hydrogen can be produced cleanly and stored safely, it's a zero-emissions vehicle. But even the fuel-cell car fails in one important respect – it's still a car.

The car has served us well, but its time will pass quite soon. Those who predict global gridlock in fifty years fail to realise that humankind's insatiable quest for movement will not stop at the new Fiat Panda any more than it stopped at the first dug-out canoe. Of course space is an issue, so rather than try to preserve that which we have, why do we not simply look to where there is still an inexhaustible supply of it? It is time to lift up our heads and cry hallelujah.

The long-term future of transport is not only personal, it's also in the air. The air offers us movement in three dimensions and, with the exception of the odd Boeing 747 or FujiFilm promotional blimp, it is completely empty. Look from the window of an aeroplane next time you're coming in to land and see just how little of the world, in pure percentage terms, is covered by roads. And yet we sense that we already have too many of them. Now look back up at the sky and see how vast it is. We can have all of that.

God knows how we will get up there freely and individually, and without a British Airways refreshing moist towelette and packet of pretzels, but we will because it is the obvious way to go. I'm not thinking of small helicopters, personal airships, flying cars or anything else that has been tried before, I'm imagining whizzing around in compact capsules elevated by some means not yet known to us. I'm imagining going from London to Manchester in a dead straight line and without even having to stop at the toll booth on the Midlands Expressway.

I realise that the physics demand something of a leap of faith, but let's face it – the logistics make complete sense. I couldn't find a parking space on my road tonight, but there's room for at least four levitating personal transport capsules on my roof, which is so far used only to store bird shit. And the air is already there for us to use, in the same way that the sea was. All we had to do was invent boats.

Who will take us to the skies? Not transport reformers, because they still see the bicycle as part of the future rather than as an early manifestation of an urge that led quite naturally to the Porsche Carrera GT. Not the environmentalists either, because they're too busy growing things. Usually on their faces.

I believe it will be our motor industry. They have the facilities, they have the research and development departments, they have an audience, they have the ready market, they have all the really brainy people and, most of all, they have the incentive. All they need to do is stop thinking of themselves simply as car makers and start thinking of themselves as – and this is how their own marketing people would put it – providers of personal transport solutions.

People tell me that new technology is spoiling the fun of driving. It isn't. It's leading us to the stars. I can't wait.

THE LAVATORY AND ITS ROLE IN THE HISTORY OF MOTORING

Anyone who reads my column regularly will know that I've never had much time for statistics. I've already demonstrated that we all have half a penis; I've since realised that I must, statistically, have one breast.

Now a friend points out that the average person must have slightly fewer than two legs, since there are some people in the mix with only one or none at all. And he's right. It's all bollocks, and I've no idea how many of those I'm supposed to have.

Still, stats are all the rage so I've come up with a few of my own.

I have calculated that, as a healthy bloke who likes a good read, I spend just over two per cent of my life on the lavvy. That doesn't sound much as a percentage, but it means in the last ten years alone I've flushed 73 days of my dwindling existence straight down the pan.

And it gets worse. As I haven't yet taken to soiling my bed at night, I have to consider that figure in relation to my waking hours, which raises the proportion to 3.1 per cent. Now there's a good chance that you're on the throne as you read this and I don't want you to labour unnecessarily with mental arithmetic, but if we assume that 75 per cent of movements occur during the working day then the downtime figure on a typical eight-hour shift becomes a significant 4.7 per cent.

So what? I hear you cry as one from the seclusion of a thousand smallest rooms all across the land. Well, if a man is going to spend that much time in the cludgey it has to be a pleasant experience, because if it isn't he will be unhappy. Unhappy people perform less well in life than contented and satisfied ones, and so, finally, we arrive at my point.

I have spent the last eight years vainly attempting to assess the output of the world's motor manufacturers on the basis of how cars perform, how well they are screwed together, how reliable they appear to be, how much they cost, how nice the interior upholstery is, and so on. I have even recently taken to talking about handling. But it's all been a waste of time. All I had to do was visit the factory and road-test the dunny. The integrity of a car manufacturer is without doubt directly related to the state of its just-in-time operations.

You know it makes sense. Let's say Mr Brown was in reception and you had the choice of travelling to France or Germany to see him out. Be honest, you'd choose Germany. I know they have those funny integral shelves for stool inspection but Jerry's plumbing is simply better than Jacques', and so, ultimately, are his cars. German plumbing is actually better than ours, which does more than any amount of financial analysis to explain how Rolls-Royce and Bentley ended up where they are today.

This makes motoring journalism much easier. In fact, anyone with a passport and a breakfast to park could do it. I once spent two weeks driving around Jordan and the Jordanians, as TE Lawrence observed, are some of the most charming and hospitable people you could ever hope to meet. They love guests almost as much as they loved the late King Hussein, the mere mention of whom can cause a hotel receptionist to break down and weep uncontrollably all over your Visa transaction.

His heir, his royal highness King Abdullah, has stated an interest in modernising and even industrialising his country. And good luck to him. He may even eventually consider making cars, but I would respectfully suggest that he does not embark on a programme of automotive development until he has sorted the nation's bogs out. For though these are exemplary within international business hotels, beyond that they represent an open passageway to Hades. Any man faced with that sort of horror for such a significant portion of his shift is not going to be completely focused on screwing your new car together.

I am utterly convinced about this. The average Jordanian outhouse immediately evoked the workers' lavatorial gulag in the GAZ automotive plant at Nizhny Novgorod, Russia, an experience I wouldn't wish upon Richard Hammond's dogs. I was barred from seeing the final production facility of this factory on the basis that 'we do not want the world to see this misery', but by then it was too late, because I'd already examined the plumbing and I had my story. I knew the Volga saloon would be pretty crappy long before I drove it.

You see, I am in the fortunate position of having visited car factories all over the world, and my theory seems to stand up very well everywhere except America, where every comfort station seems to have been specified in anticipation of a presidential visit the morning after a large doner with everything, but whose cars remain rather lacklustre.

Still works in India, though, where I once visited the Tata works. The factory thunderbox was a reasonably inviting experience and a lot better than the monument to active resistance that was the jacks in the Gandhi Memorial Park, but India in general still has some way to go on privy management. These days, fortunately, you don't need to go all the way to India to work this out. Rover's smallest car is available at your local dealer.

I've been caught short at Jaguar, Ferrari, Maserati, VW, Mercedes-Benz, Porsche and Volvo, to name a few manufacturers whose facilities are a positive incentive to buy the product. But for absolute confirmation that good cubicle equals good car, we need to go east.

To a contemplative moment snatched at Toyota's Motomachi plant in 1997, an experience so salutary that I knew at once that the Picnic MPV had been built by a workforce afforded the dignity of a proper sit-down and so would never, ever break down.

This, finally, explains the success of Japanese transplant factories in this country. It has nothing at all to do with manufacturing methods, uniforms, Japanese management techniques, the company song or the application of state aid. As with the business of international travel itself, it has everything to do with the state of the closet.

Curiously, Honda once used an advertising slogan that ran 'First man, then machine'. I think they got this wrong. It should have been 'First, karzi. Then the car.'

SOME THOUGHTS ON DRIVING ELECTRIC CARS

I would hope that, by now, you're all heartily sick of reading about the government's white paper on the future of transport. I am, especially as I've been reading the real thing.

It seems that in the future driving will be pretty much impossible, and where it is possible it will be so expensive that only pop stars and captains of industry will be able to sustain it.

I found the white paper pretty depressing. So depressing, in fact, that after a couple of hours I hurled the turgid tome out of the window and got my old Scalextric out instead.

I haven't played with my Scalextric for well over a decade. It was bought for me by some colleagues in a job I left in 1992, and following the initial burst of enthusiasm it has been left at the back of a cupboard ever since. I'd like to thank Alistair Darling for inspiring this reaquaintance with a motoring utopia in which recklessness is encouraged, accidents are to be enjoyed and a new car costs less than £30. And I know this because I immediately went out and bought two new ones to complement the Ferrari F40 and Lamborghini Diablo of the original set.

There's something deeply reassuring about Scalextric. In a world where people take photographs with mobile telephones it remains resolutely analogue and at the mercy of fluff, corrosion and cack-handed amateur soldering. There is no preferences menu, no novelty tones to down-load, no software upgrades and no personal tariffs to worry about. Scalextric is a slightly elaborate way of connecting the 12-volt DC supply from the terminals of a transformer to the carbon brushes of a small electric motor. How much more engaging O-level physics might have been if Sir had demonstrated the relationship between this simple phenom-enon and domestic motor racing. Scalextric is simply brilliant.

It's also much more dangerous than real racing. Since convention dictates that Scalextric should be assembled at floor level, and that the drivers should adopt a cross-legged position, it is a simple matter to make your Diablo fly off on a tight right-hander and strike your opponent in the wedding vegetables. This is a 'racing incident' worth half a lap at least.

And winning is easy. Simply find the speed at which your car will make it round the tightest part of the circuit and stick to it for the whole race. I tried this with my neighbour, and he was so excited about the speed at which he could pass me on the 'Mulsanne Straight' that he crashed horribly at the next bend. Then, in his eagerness to catch up again, he crashed at every bend for the remainder of the race. If you discarded the hair-trigger hand controller provided by Scalextric and substituted the rotary knob device from your train set, you could go out to dinner and come home to find your car several hundred laps in the lead.

Scalextric isn't perfect though, and its main failing is one that, a lifetime after its creation, is affecting even mainstream performance cars in the real world: too much power and too much grip.

The real Ferrari F40, for example, will cover the quarter mile from a standing start in around 12.5 seconds. I'm sad enough to have built a scale quarter mile from Scalextric track and discovered that the $1/32$nd scale F40 will do it in about 2.5 seconds. So, absurdly, will the VW Beetle. Terminal velocity (against the leg of the piano) is several hundred miles per hour.

And then there are the cornering speeds, which are so high that by the time you've realised you're losing the back end it's already too late, and, for the umpteenth time in ten minutes, you're crawling across the room to retrieve a Ferrari from under the telly. Boring.

And so, too, are a number of real cars I've been driving on real roads, and for the same reason. They have such huge tyres that cornering at anything other than insane speeds is like being guided by a slot in the road.

Fortunately, I have the solution at both levels. At the Scalextric circuit, use the train set controller to reduce power to the hand throttles by about 35 per cent. Then cover the back wheels of the cars with shiny black insulating tape bought from an electrical shop. The cars will travel at speeds your in-built hand-eye co-ordination system can compute and will never come off the track. Winning the race is now a matter of avoiding time-wasting wheelspin and oversteer through skilful use of the throttle. That's as it should be.

Meanwhile, out on the real road, this hilarious combination of low power but even lower grip is even easier to achieve. I just take my old Mini.

A GENTLEMAN DOES NOT DRIVE A DIESEL

If there's one thing that really annoys me, it's diesel engines. They're annoying in roadside generators, and they're only marginally less annoying under the bonnets of cars.

I am truly at a loss to know why society has embraced the evil genius of Dr Diesel so wholeheartedly. I realised that things had come to a head this week when Alfa Romeo started boasting that it will sell you a diesel 147 for the same price as a petrol one; that is, as cheaply. The implication here is that the diesel is a bargain because it's better. Well, I say it isn't.

I realise that the diesel engine has come a long way since the days when it powered the beige Fiesta belonging to my maths teacher. They are smoother, quieter, and much, much cleaner than they were even five years ago. Clever, too. The high-pressure injection system of a modern car diesel can provide up to five separate squirts of fuel during the twinkling of a piston that is the compression and ignition cycle, which is utterly incredible when you consider just what a brief event that is at 4000 rpm (it's happening 33 times a second, if you're interested, and half of that second is taken up with the induction and exhaust strokes).

They're economical, too, which is a weighty consideration if, like me, you find filling up pretty much the most tedious activity known to motoring kind. I also accept that their torque characteristics suit large automatics very well. And I like large automatics a lot.

But my objection to diesel is a purely spiritual one. Driving a diesel, especially a small diesel with a manual gearbox, is a bit like playing one of those miniature children's glockenspiels. Just as you think you've got a good tune going, you run out of notes.

The reasons for this are, I believe, rooted in my least favourite science – chemistry. Diesel is a slow-burning fuel compared with petrol, and it also demands a much higher compression ratio. The end result is that you don't have as many revs to play with, because the engine simply can't spin as quickly. Instead, you get more gears, and any more than five is just too baffling.

Being the sort of bloke who spends a lot of time arguing about cars in the pub, I'm ready with rapier-like ripostes to all the usual assaults from the diesel apologists, whose dronings are barely more tolerable than those from the powerplants they espouse.

Diesel is good for the motorway cruise. So? I've never driven a modern car that *isn't* good at the motorway cruise, and that includes a fuel-cell electric Vauxhall. The motorway hardly chips away at the outside of a car's dynamic envelope: there aren't even any hills to speak of. I've recently driven a Smart car on a stretch of motorway, and as it has a top speed of 84 it cruises excellently at 70. In any case, as regular readers will know, I'm trying to give up motorways because they're an affront to good automotive engineering.

Still, one fill up lasts me for 450 miles and I'm saving £40 a month over my old petrol car. This is fine if you regard motoring as a necessary evil, but I'm absolutely amazed when friends who are supposedly car enthusiasts start trumpeting the economy benefits of diesel. If there's one thing a true petrol-head shouldn't object to, it's buying petrol. Complaining about the cost of petrol is a bit like a philatelist saying 'I don't buy first-day covers because I find them too expensive. Normal stamps are much cheaper'. Note that the term 'diesel-head' is not yet in circulation.

Modern diesels have better performance than petrol cars. They've almost got me on this one, but again I return to my spiritual argument and with particular reference to the BMW 1-series, which I have been driving for the telly. The 1.6 petrol is, in all honesty, woefully slow, while the 1.8 diesel is impressively gutsy.

So the diesel has it on paper. However, on the winding roads of Wales (again) the free-spinning petrol engine, with its broad rev-range and smooth, eager nature, absolutely trounces it for this thing we call driving pleasure. Diesel power comes in great ungainly clumps, but petrol allows you to stretch out a bit. Moving from the diesel to the petrol is like coming out of solitary confinement and into a yoga class. I imagine.

Think of it this way. Diesel is stronger, but petrol is somehow fitter. The difference is like the one between a weightlifter's leg and a ballerina's.

The ballerina's is more elegant. And it will hold your attention much longer.

THE NOISE THAT ANNOYS

If there's one thing I can't stand, it's people interfering with my life. Something I can stand even less is people interfering with my life from thousands of miles away.

For example, I am writing this, at home, on a computer on which pretty much every function (apart from the one making the characters appear on the screen) has been disabled. But when I'm at the *Top Gear* office, the desktop word engine provided for me there constantly attempts to correct my grammar.

Essentially, there's a bloke somewhere in the Microsoft empire whose pedantry and smugness have been codified in digital form so that he has become as omnipotent as God, only rather less creative. He even tries to correct the spelling of some words, when he can't possibly know to spell them since I've only just made them up. It drives me mental.

A similar problem exists in the visual medium. The cameramen on *Top Gear* use very posh digital cameras packed with presets and automatic settings, but the good blokes turn all this stuff off. They reason that, in the artistry of the moment, they know best. And I think they're right. We don't want *Top Gear* made by some geek hiding in a laboratory at Sony.

This sort of thing has me wondering what happened to all the people who were studying computer programming when I was at university; during those halcyon days when the Commodore was the computer of the moment but had to be plugged into a telly and a cassette player. The best of them ended up working in research organisations, advancing the science of computing at the ragged edge of the possible. Yet more helped pioneer the Stock Market's Big Bang and the new information technology. One I knew is still employed in the design and engineering of body scanners. But this accounts only for a fraction of them.

I now realise that the remainder of them were put to work making your car more annoying.

I accept that electronic systems have done wonders for the car. They have improved engine efficiency, reduced maintenance, enhanced the effectiveness of brakes, and helped me with navigation, to take just a few examples. But now the digital tyranny is invading the cabin in a rather more pro-active way, as it does on the BBC computer, and this is less welcome. A while back I drove a Cadillac with an e-mail address. Why? I drive my car to get away from unsolicited offers of a larger penis.

The problem with digital technology is that it proliferates in a way that clockwork never could, and the result is that unnecessary functionality is added to excess. Did we learn nothing from the digital watches of the 70s? Everyone I know is now wearing something analogue.

It's bad enough when a car tells you that the driver's door is open, even though you know it is. Because you've just opened it. The noise that accompanies these intrusions makes them even more unbearable. Hundreds of years ago the musical instrument makers of Cremona perfected the timbre of a violin through little more than the selection of the wood and the formulation of the varnish, whose hardness ensured the right resonance. But the digital fraternity, with everything it has at its disposal, can manage little more than a sound like a robot belching.

And I'm afraid it's going to get worse. I've been talking to a computer scientist who says it will one day be possible to programme your sat-nav system with a profile of your 'lifestyle', so that the system will know, for example, what you like to eat and when. Then, come your regular mealtime, it can advise you in a dolorous voice that your favourite food is available three miles away, and take you there. How far will this go? Will curry enthusiasts be assailed by a virtual Indian? Those who like noodles by some sort of chip-based Chinaman? Presumably it will be able to calculate when I'm due for a trim and take me straight to Hair by Roger.

On a technical level, it's impressive. In reality, it's something else to be turned off. No one knows what you want better than you do. It's bad enough being told what to do by other people; being harangued by a car is just not on.

It's already happening. Driving the Vauxhall Monaro last week, I was subjected to a bing-bong from the bowels of the thing and a little graphic on the dash, showing a picnic table and a tree, telling me it was time for a rest stop. Says who?

I punched the dashboard somewhere and it disappeared. An easy enough solution, but I can't help feeling that something similar should have been done at the design stage. Ideally to a programmer's face.

AND LO, THE FUTURE OF THE MOTOR INDUSTRY WAS REVEALED

Sooner or later, manufacturers are going to have to turn to evangelism to sell cars. Just about everything else has been tried – the subliminal message, the naked supermodel, the implication of an enhanced lifestyle and improved sexual performance, the appeal to the ecological conscience. The intercession of the Almighty is the only truly innovative marketing tool left in the box.

Not convinced? This sort of thing is already going on in other fields, most notably in the work of the great and God-fearing American steel magnate Chuck Buck.

You've probably never heard of Chuck Buck. Neither had I until last week, when I made a pioneering trip to the North of Alaska by Land Rover. In the outdoor pursuits shop where I stocked up on ridiculous Arctic clothing I also examined a rather fine pocket knife made by Buck Knives Inc. 'Welcome aboard,' says proprietor Chuck in his intro-ductory leaflet. 'We still like to think of each one of our users as a member of the Buck Knives Family. With normal use you should never have to buy another.'

You're goddamn right, Chuck. It was perfectly balanced, beautifully made, terrifyingly sharp and curved to a fear-some-looking point. Just the job for extracting Spam from its tin in a freezing snow-drift somewhere up the notorious Dalton Highway, and as the Spam tin is these days a perfectly safe and roundy edged item, you could keep up with tradition by slicing your finger on your Buck Knife instead.

'The fantastic growth of Buck Knives Inc was no acci-dent,' continues Chuck: braces, bushy hair and the faint hint of a halo. 'From the beginning, management determined to make God the senior partner. Each knife must reflect the integrity of management, including the senior partner.' Buck knives come with a lifetime warranty, and as 'whosoever believeth in him should not perish, but have everlasting life' that's one hell of a guarantee.

All this got me thinking. It has been said by some people with beards to rival His that God rides a Harley Davidson, but I doubt it somehow. Given the slight corporate embarrassment that was the dinosaurs, it seems unlikely that He would want to be associated with anything prehistoric. No, as far as I'm aware, God does not currently hold any specific executive position within the motor industry, so assuming He has time to spare between being senior partner at Buck Knives, creator of the universe and knowing everything, a car maker should seriously consider appointing Him to the board. The first to do so is going to enjoy, like Chuck, an unassailable competitive advantage.

It will begin at factory floor level, where final-assembly technicians will work resolutely and with trembling hand lest they incur the wrath of the boss during one of his impromptu walkabouts. It will continue in the showroom, where salesmen will need no specific product knowledge or interpersonal skills whatsoever. They will simply say 'Buy this car. Or you're going to burn.' Sod cup holders and sporting pedigree – that's what I call a unique selling point.

The launch of a new car under the direction of God is going to be a, er, revelation. Instead of boring us with fatuous performance statistics and all that stuff about brand attributes, the manufacturer will simply hand us a timeless marketing concept carved on a tablet of stone and tell us to go forth and multiply. And with God on board, who's going to ask questions about airbags?

Apparently, you'll never get to heaven in an old Ford car, 'cause an old Ford car won't get that far, but a new one, conceived under the aegis of Him by whom all things were made, will lead you straight up that road paved with the earthly conceits of mortal chief executives to the pearly gates themselves, when the trumpet soundeth. Just as soon as Ford gives God a job.

Divine management has been Chuck Buck's master stroke and a classic example of that much-vaunted business technique – managing upwards. After all, if you want something doing, give it to a busy man. God, for example. 'Besides being senior partner,' quoth Chuck, 'He is our heavenly father also.' This is Chief Executive Officer J Hova Snr the first, a bloke with such a far-reaching portfolio at Buck Knives that He still has time to continue in His previous role as the immortal invisible.

Then again, it could be that Chuck Buck is the most heinous heretic this side of Satan himself and a man in dire need of salvation. Senior partner indeed. When the handle falls off a Buck knife within the span of this life, the buck will stop with Chuck and go no higher. And if I were God I think I'd want Chuck Buck to shut the f**k up. Amen.

Still, nice try. I liked the senior partner so much, I bought the product.

TWO PINTS OF LAGER AND A SMALL
HATCHBACK, PLEASE

Drink is the enemy of the motorist. Drinking and driving wrecks lives and, almost as bad, drinking causes us to talk cobblers about cars. Given two pints of warm motor-show lager in a plastic so-called 'glass', grown men will sit in a Daewoo Musso and enthuse about it. I once drank at a motor show and came home with a brochure about car ports.

The MGB enjoys an idyllic association with the country pub only because that's where people go to talk about them. No one ever drives an MGB. They're always broken, which instead drives their owners to the boozer to discuss the problem and ensures that it is not solved.

Drink has never been of any benefit to the car owner. Until now.

I have been drinking heavily over the subject of the Audi A2, a car in which my conflicting interests of beer and driving have been admirably resolved. So, pfitz! I'll have another tin.

Audi is trumpeting its new A2 as a revolution in small car design. To be honest, I'm not entirely sure it is. It looks rather interesting, it's reasonably roomy and it has the usual exemplary Audi switchgear. But the ride is a bit hard and in the end it's just a small car, and a rather expensive one starting at £13,950.

In manufacturing terms, though, it's something special because it's made largely of aluminium, the Holy Grail of mass-production automotive materials. Its body is all aluminium, formed of aluminium pressings fixed to an aluminium spaceframe fabricated from extrusions and exquisite die castings. An aluminium car is a good thing because it's light; being light means less wear on roads and tyres and less fuel consumed or, if you prefer, better performance for the same amount of it. The aluminium A2 is reckoned to weigh 43 per cent less than it would if built using steel, and aluminium is an abundant metal readily and cheaply extracted from beer tins.

How many beer tins, I wondered, as I walked home with a four-pack of John Smith's widget-equipped draught bitter, would it take to build an A2? So I drank the first one, sawed up the tin and a portion of my left index finger to remove the widget (which is plastic), and weighed it. It weighed 20 grammes.

Then I had a second tin of John Smith's and looked up the weight of the A2's spaceframe, which is 75.1kg. After another tin of Smith's I had worked out that it would take 3,755 tins to provide the raw materials for one A2 spaceframe, but not the body panels.

So what? Well, the more I drink, the more twaddle I can talk. But the more I drink, the nearer someone gets to driving a new A2. It's the exact opposite of the problem afflicting the MGB. After the final tin I had come up with the following computations, which you can check using the figures at the bottom, since I've had a few.

The volume of John Smith's that must be consumed to produce an A2 is 4,950 litres, or 8,711 pints.

If you replaced your A2 every three years and during those three years drank enough John Smith's to provide the aluminium for the entire bodyshell, you would have spent £4,500 a year on beer at current prices.

Transporting that much beer home from the supermarket would require just two round trips in an A2, with the rear seats lowered.

Enjoying a tin of John Smith's contributes 0.002234 per cent, by total weight, to the manufacture of an Audi A2.

Using your columnist as a sample, each Audi A2 represents 181 hours and 45 minutes spent standing at a urinal.

So far this is not terribly promising. Even the motoring correspondent of the *Glasgow Herald* couldn't drink him-

THE DULL RED GLOW OF TECHNOLOGY

self to a new A2. However, if we imagine a Spitfire Fund type of arrangement for the gathering of aluminium for Audi's front-line hatchback, and polish off the remains of the Scotch as well, the following figures emerge.

If every motorist in Britain drank one tin of John Smith's every day, there would be enough aluminium for an annual production of 852,276 A2s, with enough material left over for two spare spaceframes.

The actual projected production rate for the A2 demands that each British motorist drinks a tin of John Smith's only every two weeks.

I, however, can do rather better than that. What a pity I'm not in the market for an A2. Then again, as I said, drinking and driving don't mix anyway. So I'll drink, you can drive.

STATS BOX
1 tin of John Smith's £1.20
Volume of tin 440 ml
Weight of tin without widget 20 g
Weight of A2 spaceframe 75.1 kg
Weight of complete A2 body 225.0 kg
Total kerb weight of A2 895 kg
A2 luggage vol 1,085 litres
A2 production target 60,000 a year
No of UK car owners 26,268,802
May's average pee-time per pint 1 min 15 secs

NOT SO MUCH A CLOCK AS A SIGN OF THE TIMES

For some years now I have been trying to identify the point at which England was ruined. I thought it would be in the arena of politics – some aspect of foreign policy, perhaps – or maybe something sociological. But I have now discovered, rather predictably, that The Fall was heralded by our motor industry.

Let us first go back many years, to that point in my life when first I realised that I wanted a Rolls-Royce Corniche. It was an unlikely ambition for a twenty-year-old in a bright yellow MkI Vauxhall Cavalier with a stoved-in passenger's door, but the young mind is impressionable and enduringly optimistic.

I was driving along a dual carriageway in a steady flow of heavy traffic when the immaculate silver/blue fixed-head Royce, gleaming softly as if absorbing the last fading light from the embers of a doomed class system (it would have still been quite new then), approached imperiously up the adjoining slip road.

Out of instinctive deference, and having always been rather burdened by a psychological Victorian mill-worker's cloth cap and dangling forelock, I dropped back so that the glittering monument to the inequality inherent in the system (or whatever it was Eric Idle said in the Monty Python film) could join the stream of four-cylinder and ephemeral proletariat tinsel.

The driver's window, appearing grey and opaque in the low autumnal sun, slid down like mercury draining from a broken thermometer. There then emerged a beautifully gloved lady's hand, to deliver a perfectly finished wave which I saw then as one of gratitude but which I now see as a gesture laden, for all its apparent lightness, with dismissive contempt. But it was the black glove of my fate, and it smote me.

And so, yesterday, I went to look at one for sale locally. A Corniche, I mean. And I have to say my first impressions, formed over two decades ago, were absolutely right: this is surely one of the most elegant cars this country has ever produced. People are wont to dismiss the Corniche as nothing more than a two-door Silver Shadow, but it is actually something much finer. The bespoke bodywork, produced by R-R's Mulliner Park Ward workshop, is different in every detail and especially in the kink of its hips and the way its rear wings taper to those exquisite lamp lenses. The woods used in the Corniche are more exotic, the seats more fulsome, the lambswool carpet even more unfathomable. The windows, as I observed before, really do go up and down at a dignified speed.

And unlike the saloon, which looks better as the Bentley T-series I have, the Corniche is somehow better looking as a Rolls. It's something to do with the way a body, apparently inspired by the movement of water, resolves into a totally incongruous scale model of a classical Greek building at the front. It's like a beautiful woman in safety specs. They would make anyone else look like a berk, but she can somehow get away with it. But what's this?

A digital clock. There in the peerless expanse of jelutong or whatever, as 70s as a plastic-sandalled urchin on a space hopper, the legend 12:34 in slightly slanty characters, flickering greenly. What in God's name were they thinking of? If Big Ben had an LED readout and played the theme music from EastEnders it wouldn't look more inappropriate.

This is not the comedy of the Austin Maestro's synthesised voice, or the horror of the Triumph Acclaim (or Sieg Heil, as I think it was known in Germany). Those things were fleeting. But in a Rolls, an error endures as surely as the plating on the air vents.

Eventually, of course, Rolls-Royce abandoned this instrument of Satan, but that's not the point. It's not the point that it ruins this particular car, either. The point is that up until then, the people at Crewe were always far too restrained to fall for any technological red herrings. For example, by the time they had perfected their digital dashboard (not many people know this) the world had already declared such things pointless, and so it was thrown in a cupboard and forgotten. Yet somehow, the digital clock got through.

And there it was, in my favourite car, as fatuous as the red readout on that watch you bought because it appeared in the James Bond film; confirmation that Tennyson was right, that the old order had changed, yielding place to new.

How ironic that I should have found the answer to my original question in this clock, the first of which must have recorded, to the minute, the moment at which we blew it. I went home and had a long lie down.

(The author is delighted to report that the new Rolls-Royce Phantom has an analogue timepiece.)

THE GLORIOUS USELESSNESS OF INTERNAL COMBUSTION

The remarkable thing about the new Mercedes S-class, as we discussed on *Top Gear* the other day, is that for all its technological advances – its infra-red headlights, the accident avoidance technologies, the multiple massage seats – it's still powered by essentially the same means that were used to propel Benz's original Motorwagen of 1898.

I realise that the internal combustion piston engine has come a long way in the last century. The earliest ones were woeful devices: hideously inefficient and dirty by our standards, slow running, difficult to start (most people had a man for that) and, if it did start, fiendishly hard to manage. What's really amazing, though, is that the thing is still with us at all.

It strikes me that the fundamentals of the piston engine – which haven't changed one bit – must be anathema to the purist engineer. It is dependent on reciprocating motion, which is always problematic, and consumes much of the power it develops in its own operation, rather in the way that the London congestion charge spends much of the revenue it generates on its own admin. There are camshafts to be rotated, valve springs to be compressed, coolant and oil pumps to be driven, electrical sparks to be generated. I'm sitting here looking at a cutaway drawing of a Porsche flat six, and I'm amazed at just how little of the mechanism is directly related to driving the car. The rest of it is devoted, as management types would say, to making it happen.

A jet engine is so much better, since (in essence, anyway) everything rotates smoothly and efficiently around a central shaft. And yet, despite one or two dramatic attempts, the gas turbine has never given us a quantum leap in car performance in the way that it has for aeroplanes.

War must have a lot to do with this, since it tends to encourage advances in aviation while leaving cars up on bricks owing to fuel shortages. The driver of a 30s Bentley could drive the new Continental Flying Spur, once he'd got over the shock of discovering that the gear lever is indoors. The pilot of a Hawker Hurricane wouldn't even know which way to face in the Eurofighter. Then compare the performance improvements of both: the car's would be expressed in percentages, but the aeroplane's in multiples.

So the engine in your car is beginning to look a bit rubbish, really. Everything else has moved on. Aeroplanes have gas turbines; ships have gas turbines and nuclear reactors; railways have had diesel electric, diesel hydraulic, turbines, pure electric and MagLev. I know we now have hybrid cars, but let's not kid ourselves about these: they are still driven entirely by petrol or diesel, and the electric motor and its associated systems are merely there in an attempt to recoup some of the energy the piston engine so famously wastes.

Think about this. The most important industry in the world, the purveyors of the most expensive consumer artefact most of us ever buy, the cornerstone of world economies, the ambassador for nations, the motor industry: still fobbing you off with lumps of metal flapping about in holes inside other great big lumps of metal. We ought to be pretty cross about it.

However, I've decided that I'm delighted.

I've been thinking about engines quite a bit over the last few weeks, and it has to be acknowledged that it's the deficiencies of the technology that make them so exciting. There has never been a truly great car with a dull engine, because the engine, as Ferrari are so keen to point out, is the soul of the car.

Imagine a perfect petrol engine, with absolutely linear responses, a smooth torque curve, an even sound through-out the rev range. How boring would that be? We look at graphs of engine output and tut at troughs in the torque, but let's be honest: this is exactly the sort of thing that makes it interesting in daily operation.

Even the least mechanically sympathetic driver is intimately in tune with the workings of the engine: when it's labouring, when it's straining. This is a vital part of the feedback at the man/machine interface and as crucial as steering feel to the sort of people who really enjoy driving.

A few cars I've driven in the last week or so stand as a perfect illustration of what I'm talking about: a Porsche Boxster, my old Bentley, and Hammond's knackered 1275cc MG Midget. These three are about as disparate as you could get, yet all offer an opportunity to delight in the foibles of the piston engine.

The Midget has a pretty woeful old lump under its shuddering bonnet. It offers nothing at low revs and runs out of puff suddenly, and just before you expect it to. But this is something you recognise within a few miles of driving, and life beyond that point is a hilarious game of hunting down that fleeting period of the engine's operating range when it comes 'on the cam' and keeps the little box bowling along. It's everything a milk float isn't, despite a similar performance envelope.

The 3.2 flat six in the new Boxster S is a much more sophisticated affair, offering complex electronic control, variable valve timing and everything else possible in the pursuit of that theoretically perfect motor mentioned above. But of course they will never actually get there, which means that there is a beautiful sweet spot in the engine, at about 4,000 revs and under load, when its workings translate to a curious tingle in the base of the spine. This is felt on driving out of a perfectly executed corner and is as enduringly satisfying as ejaculation.

The Bentley? Hardly a thrilling powerplant in the accepted sense. It's all over by 4,500 rpm and its makers made every effort to banish its sound completely. And yet . . . that great swelling of torque as you pull away, and the distant aristocratic harrumph from the bowels of the thing; these serve to remind you that you are ministering to a mass of whirling ironmongery fuelled by countless explosions, flawed but magical.

Oh – just remembered: I've driven one other car recently, a fuel-cell Vauxhall Zafira, a true electric car with its own on-board power station. The fuel cell sits where the regular engine would – it's even on the same mountings. The technology works brilliantly, and in time it could be made cheaply, since it's simple and simple to use: no gearbox, no stalling, no cussed torque characteristics. Just press the pedal and go on your way with a faint whine, quietly, cleanly and efficiently. This is almost certainly the future, and I have only one complaint about it.

God in heaven, it's boring.

CONCLUSION

HERE ARE A FEW I DIDN'T QUITE MANAGE TO FINISH EARLIER

Like most people these days, I own a CD player but, unlike many of my friends, I have never quite been able to give up my collection of proper records.

The other day, though, I was listening to an old and much-loved pop album from my youth – let's say, for argument's sake, it was *Second That Emulsion* by Matt Vinyl and the Undercoats – and I had to acknowledge that it was utterly worn out. So, as you'd expect, I went out and bought a replacement copy, on CD.

And at first it was fine. It sounded exactly like the record but without the scratches, and I could let it play away in the background without keeping half an ear cocked for the build-up of tumbleweed on what I still like to call the 'needle'. But then it all went horribly wrong.

Where the original album finished, this one continued with alternative recordings of well-known tunes and a few bonus tracks; all stuff that, under the tyranny of the supposedly 'long-playing' record, would have been chucked in the bin. Rightly, in my view.

Then I watched a film on one of those DVD players. Again, it was a familiar work and at first it went just as I remembered it. But then I was treated to some unused scenes, director's cuts and other bits that, had they been celluloid, would be on the floor somewhere, where they belong.

The digital media have unleashed a terrible demon into popular culture, namely the out-take. Stuff that should have been discarded in the ruthless process of creativity is now seen as a marketable commodity to make overpriced CDs and DVDs look like better value. Where will it end? Soon Terry Wogan will be hosting a Christmas TV show called *Auntie's Bloomers' Bloomers*, in which we are subjected to an hour of cutting-room detritus showing the great man making a cock-up of the job of presenting cock-ups.

So I've decided to cash in. On my computer is a rather tragic file marked 'Ideas', full of all the things that never quite worked, or that went wrong, or that didn't have the legs to fill the page, or that in some other way expose the soft and endearingly human underbelly of this great inventive genius, as is fashionable. Here, then, are the James May Late-Night Sessions, a selection of previously unprinted and never-before-read fragments from my own forgotten archive of absolute crap. Remember – these bonus paragraphs would not be available if I were still using a typewriter.

The other day I set off on a long car journey but, ten miles from home, realised I'd forgotten my road atlas. But then I saw the sign for Alton Towers and realised that I wouldn't need it anyway.

For every genuinely useful directional road sign there is a brown one pointing the way to some fatuous tourist attraction. But soon they will become useful to the navigationally challenged, because so much of the country is now some sort of visitors' centre that it will soon be possible to plot a course from one place to another blah blah blah

blah cobblers. See if it's poss to navigate from London to the *Scotland on Sunday* office using only the brown tourist signs instead of real ones. Remember to include bloke with the snake sanctuary who has a brown zoo sign showing outline of an elephant because that's what the EC demands or something.

Jag's indicators – make a nice woody noise everyone comments on it. Think of some other little things in cars that make a nice noise or feel good. Do these things affect the way we remember a car? Also Skoda knobs etc. (DONE!! 18/3/01)

Corporate clothing – what goes with what car? Start with freebie Land Rover boots – good for grip and off-roading, like car. Choose other cars and suggest appropriate clothing.

Bullitt is bunk – why does everyone go on about it being a great film when really it's a pretty mediocre film with a quite good car chase in it? Ford Mustang. Ring Ford for details also that Steve McQueen ad for the Puma. Get film out on video and make notes.

Jag handbook – rewrite the driving advice section for different markets, showing how different habits have to be accommodated, like stuff about roundabouts for France, stuff on dangers of smoking when filling up, not applicable in Italy etc etc.

The danger of talking like Jeremy Clarkson.

Decline of the Great British roadside burger caravan, re that one up the dual carriageway been banished by the council. On next long drive use backroads and take in as many caravans as poss. Start campaign to preserve our burger heritage, bring down Little Chef. Invite nominations for Britain's best roadside bacon roll. Extra cheese go way of sausage etc. Maybe burger map of Britain for sales reps and truckers, so people can navigate between them. See also brown road signs above.

Why motor industry marketing people are all stupid.

275

An Apology

This column, in tandem with the motoring sections of numerous other national newspapers and certain sectors of the specialist motoring press, may in previous weeks have given the impression that John Prescott is a fat fool and the enemy of the British motoring public.

We would like to point out that any such impression is entirely at odds with Mr Prescott's true character, and that no offence or slur on his name was ever intended.

Continue like this, as if in support of JP, but at the same time carefully reiterating view that he is a threat to society. Finish with something about fear of being punched.

SOURCES

Car Magazine
'Some hot air ...' (September 2005) 'Germans victorious
...' (July 1995) 'Ah, Mr Bond ...' (August 1998) 'Motor-
way services ...' (Jan 1996) 'Jesus Christ ...'(January
1995) 'This man's driving...' (August 1997) 'Racing to the
...' (July 1998) 'Wanted: graduate trainee ...' (July 1996)
'Where we will be ...' (February 2004) 'The Mazda ...'
(December 1998) 'Learning to drive ...' (March 1997)
'Love for Sale ...' (June 1998) 'The people's crisp ...'
(November 1998) 'The soft underbelly ...' (November
1997) 'Kicked in the nuts ...' (September 1997) 'Fortunately the past ...' (October 1995) 'A lifetime in ...' (August
1995) 'He's terribly British ...' (August 1998) 'The old of
today ...' (June 1996) 'I met ...' (March 1999).

Top Gear
'The train now departing ...' (March 2001) 'If you like to
gamble ...' (February 2004) 'All you need to know ...'
(March 2004) 'Land Rover ...' (January 2004) 'Some
blue-chip bullshit ...' (July 2001) 'Car accessories ...'

(January 2005) 'Sheep . . .' (December 2004) 'The Lavatory
. . .' (August 2004).

Daily Telegraph

'Turn on, tune in . . .' (November 2003) 'This precious car
. . .' (September 2004) 'Welsh, the mystical . . .' (April 2004)
'I can drive a Ferrari . . .' (May 2004) 'Tools . . .' (September 2004) 'I am not an executive . . .' (February 2004) 'Got
a garage . . .' (March 2004) 'A bad case . . .' (June 2004)
'The journey's only . . .' (February 2004) 'The dustbin of
automotive . . .' (October 2003) 'For Pete's sake . . .' (May
2004) 'What the motor industry . . .' (January 2004) 'Some
thoughts on driving . . .' (July 2004) 'Motor industry suffers
. . .' (March 2004) 'A right merry ding-dong . . .' (November 2004) 'A gentleman . . .' (November 2004) 'The noise
. . .' (October 2004) 'Dangerous dogs . . .' (March 2005)
'All the nuts . . .' (August 2004) 'Buying a house? . . .'(April
2005) 'The busy man's guide . . .' (February 2005) 'How the
men . . .' (June 2004) 'Puff Daddy . . .' (May 2004) 'The
brown movement . . .' (October 2003) 'We all live . . .'
(October 2004) 'How Porsche ruined . . .' (February 2005)
'I put my money . . .' (April 2004) 'Seeking something . . .'
(July 2004).

Scotland on Sunday

'Now is the winter . . .' (January 2001) 'And you thought
. . .' (July 2000) 'Dead cars . . .' (March 2000) 'Germany
invades . . .' (October 2000) 'Ours are bad . . .' (April 2000)
'Here are a few . . .' (June 2001) 'One day I . . .' (June 2000)
'Everything you need . . .' (January 2000) 'Charity begins
. . .' (October 2000) 'Volvo drivers . . .' (August 1999) 'And
lo . . .' (November 2000) 'Cycle your way . . .' (April 2001)
'Two pints of lager . . .' (August 2000) 'Aluminium commodity . . .' (September 2000) 'Ask me . . .' (August 2000).

INDEX